PREACHING TO PROGRAMMED PEOPLE

*Effective
Communication
in a
Media-Saturated Society*

D1235004

PREACHING TO PROGRAMMED PEOPLE

Effective Communication in a Media-Saturated Society

TIMOTHY A. TURNER

kregel
RESOURCES

Grand Rapids, MI 49501

Preaching to Programmed People
by Timothy A. Turner

Copyright © 1995 by Timothy A. Turner

Published by Kregel Resources, a division of Kregel, Inc., P.O. Box 2607, Grand Rapids, MI 49501. Kregel Resources provides timely and relevant resources for Christian life and service. Your comments and suggestions are valued.

Cover artwork: Photodisc, vol. 1
Cover and book design: Alan G. Hartman

Library of Congress Cataloging-in-Publication Data

Turner, Timothy A., 1949–
  Preaching to programmed people: effective communication in a media-saturated society / by Timothy A. Turner.
     p.   cm.
  Includes bibliographical references.
  1. Preaching. Television broadcasting—Religious aspects—Christianity. I. Title.
BV4211.2.T88   1995   251—dc20   95-8718
                                           CIP

ISBN 0-8254-3849-7 (pbk.)

     1 2 3 4 5 printing / year 99 98 97 96 95

Printed in the United States of America

To
Hannah
Matthew
Abby
Rachel.
and especially Mary Lou, my wife

Also special thanks to—
Ruth, Paul and Carol, Ginger, Jana, Judy, Patty, and
Ramona, my sister, for typing manuscript revisions

And to Jack Simons for his insight and encouragement

And to Dennis Hillman and Helen Bell
at Kregel Publications for their support
and analysis of the issues.

For speaking and conference
information, write or call:

Tim Turner
Media & Ministry
7252 So. Meridian St.
Marion, IN 46953
(317) 674–4760

Contents

PART I
What Has TV Done to Preaching?

PART II
What Should Preaching Do About TV?

Foreword

D r. Turner has alerted us in a specific way to a problem we have all sensed and wondered about—TV has all but taken over our culture! The problem is known, but few have responded to it. Dr. Turner has done just that. In very readable and practical terms he cites data, explains the problem in terms we can get a hold on, and suggests ways preachers can do something to solve it. You owe it to yourself and your congregation to read and consider what he says. This is not a mere discussion; you will find help here that has been used profitably by others before you. The need for this book is real.

Perhaps several pastors in an area could read the book and then discuss it, using it as a catalyst for raising additional ideas. Buy it; you'll be glad you did.

JAY ADAMS

Simsonville, SC
1995

What Has TV Done to Preaching?

CHAPTER ONE

TV Has "Captured" Your Congregation

P lace yourself in this scene. It's Sunday morning and the services have just ended. As you're standing in the foyer of your church, shaking hands and thanking your people as they leave, your eye picks up a blur of bodies streaking out the side door. The teenagers who sat in the back counting ceiling boards, stuffing the communion cup holders full of chewing gum wrappers, and passing notes to each other written on visitor cards during your sermon duck out the side door to avoid you.

At home they tell their parents, "Our pastor is boring. His sermons are dull and impossible to understand! Why do we have to go to church anyway?" You are fully aware that these same teenagers sit for more than twenty-six hours each week held captive by television. Even Archimedes and his lever couldn't separate them. The contrast is too painful to ignore.

Then you hear a soft and gentle voice, "Thank you, Pastor, for that fine sermon." Sadly you recall that this sweet, elderly lady nodded off to dreamland several times before the sermon ended. The elderly lady is experiencing the unavoidable negative effects of the aging process which are only intensified by TV, since its viewers remain in a physically frozen position for hours on end. Yet, women above the age of fifty-five consume more TV than any other age group, watching nearly forty-one hours of TV each week.

Abruptly you feel something squeezing your hand and see your arm acting like a pump handle as Bob and Claudia, a committed Christian couple, shake your hand and introduce you to a nonchurched friend they

> "Facing the facts means admitting that the people to whom you preach have a love affair with TV."

have finally succeeded in bringing to the service. Their guest responds politely but gives you the impression that he would rather be watching the sports reviews on channel 4. He'll probably never return.

In the silent foyer you prepare to go home when a godly church leader approaches and attempts to encourage you about this year's slump in church attendance. "People just don't want to hear sound teaching anymore, Pastor. These are the last days you know."

Do these scenes look familiar? They should—I've experienced each of them myself, and so have thousands of other pastors.

Everyone we've just met must now hurry home to rush through lunch in order to fall asleep while watching the afternoon ball games. The same scenes are played out again after the evening service, except instead of sports programs the rush is on for something like *Murder, She Wrote.*

The people in the examples above attend your church. They consume TV almost nonstop. Facing the facts means admitting that the people to whom you preach have a love affair with TV.

For example, teenagers watch more than twenty-three hours each week. By the time young people in America today graduate from high school, they have spent more than 17,500 hours in front of their sets compared to only 13,500 hours in the classroom. That the working man should watch more TV than the typical teenager seems strange, but it is undeniably true. Adding sports, news, and other prime-time fare together amounts to twenty-six hours forty-four minutes in front of the tube for men ages twenty-five to fifty-four. But the heaviest users of all are women over fifty-five who view nearly forty hours per week, followed closely by preschoolers who view cartoons twenty-six hours during that same period.

Why do people watch so much TV? The answer is simple—it pervades our culture. By any measuring stick, it has eclipsed its rival media in revenues and power. Radio, newspapers, books, and magazines are no longer equal competitors with TV. On a daily basis only 35 percent of Americans read a newspaper and only 45 percent listen to the radio. TV is the dominant form of communication in America today and has been for nearly twenty years.

Ninety-eight percent of American homes have a TV; 64 percent have two or more. In 1991 alone Americans purchased over 21.5 million color sets. On an average the TV runs 29.5 hours per week in the home. Even its location exhibits authority. The glass box positions itself in the living room as the oval office of the family—TV dominates Americans' minds and homes.[1]

In 1977 the noted British media expert Malcolm Muggeridge said, "TV is the greatest single influence in society today."[2] Since then it has tightened its grip on America twofold. For these reasons it has been dubbed the third superpower and the fourth member of the Trinity. Clearly, omnipotent TV holds our hearers in a viselike grip.

Of what significance are these statistics to you and your preaching? In what ways has a lifetime of exposure to TV by average adults in your congregation altered their responses to your preaching? Does a craving for TV make people uneasy with preaching? How else can we explain why people who log thousands of hours absorbing TV find it less-than-gratifying to listen to one hour of preaching? We know that TV consumption hinders our ability to *read*— declining SATs prove this fact. But does it cast its same crippling shadow over our ability to *listen* to preaching?

Since radio, newspapers, and magazines—all part of the communication world—have been reshaped by TV, it is unlikely that preaching has escaped TV's awesome influence. TV covers America like rain. Who believes preaching escapes the downpour?

Pastors, like Martha in the Bible, experience anxiety and trouble about many things, so why should we be especially concerned about media's influence on preaching? Here are four good reasons:

1. TV hinders preaching, the heart of the church.

In a recent survey of two hundred churches the number one reason people stayed in a church was not the music ministry, the youth group, or even the church's friendliness. Although guests attended initially for a variety of reasons, the number one reason they remained was the preaching.[3] Anything that hinders effective preaching is injurious to the health and growth of the church. Simply put, TV hinders effective preaching.

2. TV competes with preaching.

TV competes with preaching in the business of communication. In fact, any preacher not in the communication business goes out of business. Because TV dominates our culture and judges all other forms of communication by its standard, we preach in its flickering shadow.

3. TV offers a commercial—not eternal—message.

Both TV and preaching seek to reach the same people with a very different message—one commercial, the other eternal. Yet we're both competing for the same audiences.

4. TV seeks to change its listeners.

Possibly the most strategic comparison of all is that both TV and preaching seek to change their listeners in some substantial way. The media elite tell us that their stated goal is to move viewers toward their view of social reform and not just to make money.[4]

These decisive questions and concerns call for equally cogent solutions. This book will help you preach to your TV-conditioned congregation. In the following chapters we will "fine tune your focus" on special areas such as:

- the way TV changes how people hear, analyze, and respond to your preaching
- the most forceful length for sermons
- the legitimate use of commercials in your sermons
- how to structure your sermons for maximum impact

> "Because TV dominates our culture and judges all other forms of communication by its standard, we preach in its flickering shadow."

Many, if not all, of those flagging parishioners can be revived by preaching that not only overcomes but capitalizes on TV-conditioning. Pastor, take heart! Criticism about dull or boring preaching in the past can be changed!

You may ask, "Can you tell me how to preach to people who are so hooked on TV that they fall asleep during my introduction or to people who think that my sermon is a failure if it isn't short, sweet, and entertaining?"

Yes! is the answer to these questions. There is hope for penetrating even your most hardened TV-conditioned listeners. The purpose of this book is to enable you to preach effectively to media-saturated people.

CHAPTER TWO

The TV-Conditioned Mentality

I have suggested that the molding power of TV has adversely affected your congregation's Sunday morning preaching experience. It has, in fact, implanted in the people of your church a TV-conditioned mentality that constitutes a genuine barrier to effective preaching. How did this barrier arise?

Preaching's New Breed of Listeners

Having preached nearly every Sunday for twenty-five years and discussed preaching issues with preachers across the country, I offer this observation. There is an uneasy feeling among preachers that something about preaching has changed over the past ten to fifteen years. Subtly, an almost imperceptible something is different. It is not the Bible or the way most preachers approach their task. What then? The people sitting in the pews? Yes, many things about them have changed—their understanding of what a sermon is and should do, their understanding of the roles and relationships that define the preacher-listener model, their understanding of the preacher's job, and their understanding of their expectations as hearers in the overall process of the preaching event. Their former assumptions about the preaching paradigm have changed.

Consider the old preaching model that defined the role and relationship between preacher and people in evangelical churches of America twenty years ago. The preacher expected to deliver a straightforward and content-laden message from the Bible. How long, how entertaining, or how relevant to everyday living the sermon was were either secondary or inconsequential. Hearers came to church with a sober-minded sense of responsibility to pay attention to and to concentrate on the sermon; this expectation included sitting still, staying quiet, and focusing on the message regardless of whether or not the sermon was effortless to hear or enjoyable to experience. Such expectations between pastor and people were mutually understood and relatively well defined. In some churches, no doubt, this same model may still exist.

On a wider scale today, however, such notions have been replaced by the new media-engendered model of the 1990s. No longer are these former assumptions valid. We now preach to the mentality of the '90s where such issues as attention span, relevance of the message, and listener involvement call for reconsideration. A new breed of hearers have redefined the preacher-listener paradigm. What precipitated this shift?

The Influence of TV

On the average, every adult in your congregation between the ages of twenty-five and forty has watched thirty to forty thousand hours of TV. Our society is the first in human history to devote itself so exclusively to one form of communication to the relative exclusion of other forms. This extraordinary chunk of time Americans spend under the influence of TV has left its imprint. Consequently, preaching today faces the challenge of a new breed of hearers who expect easy, effortless, and even entertaining communication.[1] The old preacher-hearer roles and relationships have given way to the new media-engendered model. (No, we can't saddle TV with the entire load of blame; however, within the complex interaction between media and culture it deserves a lion's share.)

After watching nearly thirty hours of TV each week people handily and thoughtlessly transfer these entertainment expectations to the preaching service Sunday morning. But because of TV's power to change the way people hear, analyze, and respond to spoken communication, preaching is a letdown. This letdown occurs for at least two reasons.

First, the mental skills, listening aptitudes, and spiritual sensitivity necessary for people to benefit from preaching are light years removed from the typical couch-potato mentality that celebrates being "glued to the tube" in some mindless zombielike state of mind. TV requires less concentration, less effort, and is much more entertaining than preaching. To get anything out of preaching requires a set of more stringent abilities that includes listening, thinking, and staying focused instead of mentally wandering off into oblivion. People who acquire a taste for TV prove unlikely to develop the capabilities needed to hear preaching.

Second, the listener's role in hearing preaching and the viewer's role in watching TV bear little resemblance to each other. People often say they "watch TV," but they don't say they "watch" the preacher—they say they "listen" to him. These testimonies reflect the corresponding differences which each form imposes. Because TV and preaching are antithetical forms of communication, their rivalry creates a like antagonism between the roles of the viewer and listener. When watching TV, one must conform to the viewer role that TV assigns; when listening to a preacher, one must listen carefully and sensitively to the spiritual content of the message.

Well-known among media experts and largely ignored among preachers, the requirements prescribed by differing forms of communication are so powerful they can change the audience, the message, and the even the communication process itself.[2] Consider their differences.

Forms That Fight

Preaching and TV employ forms of communication that fight. Contrast the visual-image-centered communication of TV with the verbal and imageless content of preaching. TV is word poor and preaching is word rich. In TV words are secondary, in preaching they're everything. Any pictures in preaching must be created by the only tools the preacher has—words. Such differences are equivalent to a war between words and pictures. This dichotomy between forms causes a necessary divergence in appeal. So a second and more crucial difference exists.

TV is sensual in appeal, whereas preaching is rational in approach. Sensual appeal doesn't necessarily mean sinful appeal, but simply that TV charms our senses. It allures the eyes and ears; mentally reflecting on all one sees and hears is incidental. Like doors and windows, the organs of sight and sound serve only to channel the message into the mind.

Preaching, however, as rational communication, approaches the mind with words instead of images and must succeed in penetrating the hearer's *understanding* or it fails. Most listeners cease to listen when they cease to comprehend. A similar failure to understand what they watch on the part of TV viewers would be of little or no consequence. Viewers continue to watch regardless of their understanding. To understand TV is a concept foreign in itself. Viewers reach their goal of being entertained by watching, not by understanding.

What does preaching offer the senses by comparison—the background behind the pulpit, the choir loft, the preacher's attire? These pale by comparison to TV and often actually steal from the preacher's message instead of give strength to it. Rarely can a person focus on the appearance of the church and preacher and the content of

"As a communication form, language, as opposed to images, must function on a higher, more energy-intensive plane. It requires activity, effort, and time on the part of the receiver to follow, process, comprehend, and respond. When a preacher uses words, therefore, he automatically aims at the mind as opposed to the impulses."

the sermon all at the same time. The reward of preaching is the gift of understanding. Little reward is offered to the senses.

TV, on the other hand, appeals to the mind through sights and sounds which bypass the thinking process and thereby delete any need for rational or verbal analysis. No time or effort is required for a mere glance at a sizzling steak to elicit a mouth-watering response or, likewise, for TV's lifelike pictures to evoke instantaneous lust. Substantial evidence from scientific research suggests that these differences are based in the neurology of the brain itself.[3]

Research confirms that while images process and integrate in the right hemisphere of the brain, words and print are handled in the left hemisphere. Thus there is an actual neurological distinction in the brain between watching TV and listening to preaching. This distinction made by the brain may provide the underlying rationale for why this antagonism is so intense.

This research is confirmed by Marshal McLuhan in his book, *The Medium Is the Message,* where he documents that the brain adjusts itself to the medium of the communication. Irrespective of the content, the brain decides how to process data based on the identity of the data's *form* so that different forms, such as images and words, are handled differently and consequently obtain different results. Preachers can't afford to overlook the significance of McLuhan's conclusions.[4]

In a noble attempt to grapple with this antagonism between opposing forms, Quentin Schultze, in his book, *Redeeming Television,* offers the following solution:

> The critical viewer of television has the difficult job of translating the tube's images into words. Then the words can be processed by the viewer's mind, evaluated, and discussed with other viewers.[5]

This telling advice proves impossible to follow. Undeniably, images need translation into words before discussion, but to implement this task is nearly hopeless. Anyone may easily prove this point by trying it. Hours of personal experience teach that at best it's frustrating and at worst, a nightmare. Moving images resist translation into words. TV entertains, relaxes, or offers escape but seldom evaluates or analyzes, so the medium itself, as well as its form, argues against Schultze's kind of critical analysis. However, in the same way that TV must, before discussion, undergo translation into words, so also must our hearers, before they can take in preaching, make the transition from image-centered to word-centered communication. The difficulty of this transition, as Schultze points out, explains why TV-conditioning harms preaching.

As a communication form, language, as opposed to images, must function on a higher, more energy-intensive plane. It requires activity, effort, and time on the part of the receiver to follow, process, comprehend, and respond. When a preacher uses words, therefore, he automatically aims at the mind as opposed to the impulses. To grasp this distinction is crucial. Yet this antagonism stretches beyond form to include other dissimilarities as well.

Diverse Settings

The overall TV experience falls out of line with the preaching setting. The private atmosphere within a living room, den, or bedroom where most people watch TV individually or in groups of two or three defies comparison to a public auditorium where one must sit in one spot and stand, speak, or move only when told.

The TV-watching atmosphere is casual and contains few restraints. Whenever you wish to speak, eat, move, or whatever, you can. Preaching is formal by comparison, restrictive, even tense. These differences affect how your TV- conditioned listeners hear or don't hear your preaching. Widespread indolence, scuffling, and inattention in the pew may be more of TV's dreadful legacies to our listeners who have come to church but who have failed to make the transition between these divergent settings.

Other differences separate preaching and TV watching such as the solitary (and often monotone) sound of the preacher's voice compared to TV's multitude of sounds, its endless and bizarre variety of content, and its twenty-four hour accessibility. Like David and Goliath, from the human standpoint the contrast is obvious. Preaching gets weighed in TV's balances and is found wanting.

After watching TV for thousands of hours, the brain conforms to a TV-conditioned mentality just as comfortable, well-used, old shoes conform to our feet.

CHAPTER THREE

TV Refashions People

TV changes people. But how? If people really are captured and conditioned by TV, then it's only logical to question the results. If such changes affect how people hear, analyze, or respond, they would have direct impact on a pastor's effectiveness in preaching.

By modifying the role of the audience, TV refashions its viewers and creates them in its own image. On opposite ends of the communications spectrum, the roles of the TV viewer and the preaching listener tend to be mutually exclusive. Advancing toward the one removes us by that much from the other. As a consequence of becoming comfortable with TV, we feel less at ease with preaching. This discomfort eventually develops into an antagonistic gap. A comparison of the two roles will explain how TV recasts its viewers into its own mold.

Antagonistic Roles

Our focus concerns the roles of those who hear, analyze, and respond to both TV and preaching, and why these two very different kinds of communication alter those roles.

Any process of communication can be examined on at

least three levels. First is the receptial level which involves the way we receive input from the source. This level covers areas such as setting, content, and our prevailing attitudes. Next comes the level of analysis, the methods and mental processes we use to manipulate the data. Finally, after receiving and analyzing the message, we respond. This level defines the ways this process affects us. Communication may evoke a variety of responses—thoughts, emotions, actions, or attitudes.

The Receptial Level: Watching vs. Listening

As we compare viewing TV with listening to preaching, obvious contrasts mark the receptial level of the person involved. The expectations that the viewer or hearer brings to the communication event are different. One's approach to *Late Night with David Letterman,* for example, would differ from "Early Morning with Pastor Smith." One event is entertainment, the other is worship—just as *Monday Night Football* calls for a different frame of mind than "now open your Bibles to Genesis." The relaxed attitude of entertainment contrasts with the serious atmosphere of worship. Those largely accustomed to entertainment often regard worship as overly solemn and uncomfortable. By using a light-hearted, more TV-compatible mood, some contemporary forms of worship seek to narrow this gap.

Secondly, the TV-experience transforms its subjects into image-oriented watchers, while preaching demands word-oriented listeners. After hour upon hour of scrutinizing moving images that race across the screen, TV viewers learns to follow pictures that jump, wiggle, and flux by the second. They become image oriented—hence, viewers. Words dominate preaching, however, and the role of the receiver is hearing instead of watching. People can't watch spoken words. So, with preaching, people must become word-oriented hearers. Therefore, forms (images vs. words) dictate roles (watchers vs. hearers). Since to follow and to comprehend different forms people must adapt to them, differing communication forms mandate different roles. This fundamental dissimilarity generates sharp discord. This is why TV watching develops roles that are antagonistic toward preaching.

The Analysis Level: Feeling vs. Thinking

Differences every bit as striking exist on the analysis level. As we have shown, pictures tend to by-pass conscious analysis and elicit direct emotional responses without prior listening and reflecting. For example, imagine a car crash scene with blood spilled over a roadway or picture a malnourished infant with contorted features and protruding cheek bones poised to puncture holes in its face. Do these words conjure up feelings of revulsion, abhorrence, or sympathy? If so, it's because you read and comprehended them and supplied your own mental images depicting the scenes. You then reacted emotionally to what your mind pictured. Pictures evoke feelings—the more vivid the scene the more intense the feelings. If those words failed to call up the images, your emotions probably remained unstirred.

Because images create feelings *before* analysis, watching TV is not primarily a thinking but rather a feeling experience made up of laughing, crying, fearing, worrying, and so forth. Tension, not reflection, flows through one's body during a violent TV scene. Watching murder, rape, arson, and immorality spills out adrenaline, not reason. Yet, because TV dispatches rapid fire images in such haste, time exists only for the most superficial reflection. Anyone desiring to meditate on images must visit an art gallery.

For these reasons, TV moves its viewers toward a feeling, not a thinking, mentality—toward emotion over analysis—and thus hinders the hearers in our congregations from performing the necessary thinking and analyzing necessary to grasp preaching. With preaching, however, thinking must precede emotion. Preaching should not generate emotion without reason or feelings not founded on truth. This is not a plea for drab, Spock-type sermons, but a caution about the desire for an instant zap in preaching like viewers experience with TV. The analysis of preaching requires persistent concentration rather than instant gratification.

What does preaching require of its listeners at the analysis level? Is this different than TV? Jesus repeatedly challenged His followers to "hear the Word." Luke called the Bereans noble because they examined the Scriptures to see if they were true. But it is impossible for the hearer to examine Scripture without thinking about, analyzing, and comprehending the message. Such procedures and the power to carry them out are essential to any successful analysis of spoken communication. With watching TV, however, these procedures are not only incidental but largely detrimental. TV makes superfluous these very things that preaching requires.

The Response Level: Chronic Inertia

The greatest divergence between the TV and the preaching models exists at the listener's response level. Experts in communication have devised an "information-action ratio" which measures the likelihood of data to generate action.[1] Think about it—when was the last time you saw anything on TV that demanded action? Other than an occasional weather report alerting a driver to leave early because of heavy snow or traffic, the main action TV generates is buying a product which may or may not be potentially helpful. Even the prevalence of news, talk, and sports programming requires little or no action from its viewers.

Information requiring no response fosters idleness and passivity and results in brain dead listeners. They have already decided to do nothing about what they're going to hear before they even begin to listen. Widespread apathy toward preaching is only worsened by this dreadful legacy from TV which furthers an attitude of "more information I'll never use or share."

Preaching that changes lives must generate action and avoid meaningless, non-content-related responses. Listeners must respond to preaching differently! Every biblical sermon invites its hearers to *do* something, *believe* something, or *decide* some-

> "TV automatically switches every viewer into a kind of artificial mode of response. It isn't rational to respond to imaginary, fictional events as if they were real. In the same way, it is neither rational nor safe for those who listen to our preaching to respond to the real events about which we preach as if they were fiction."

thing. If our hearers are to be changed by the Truth, then indolence is intolerable. But TV-conditioned mentalities treat preaching passively since a passive response is the standard response with TV.

This fundamental dissonance exists because TV deals largely with entertainment while preaching treats real life where responses are required. Unless fiction links itself in some way to reality (which is seldom the case), TV automatically switches every viewer into a kind of artificial mode of response. It isn't rational to respond to imaginary, fictional events as if they were real. In the same way, it is neither rational nor safe for those who listen to our preaching to respond to the real events about which we preach as if they were fiction.

A cartoon of a frantic father changing a flat tire in the pouring rain helps illustrate this point. While his two children shout something from inside the minivan, the father barks back this irritated retort, "You don't understand, I can't change the channel, this is real!"

This illustration is not far-fetched. Consider the strange reality reversal TV fosters in Christian homes. Here real family members shed real tears over a fictional family's woes on TV while remaining ice-hearted toward their own family and unchurched neighbors. Preachers attempting to motivate listeners to shed real tears for real spiritually-lost people often experience a fictional response toward those awaiting the grimmest reality of all. TV viewers see so many fictional programs that their actual daily lives take on a fictional quality while the TV world seems real. The apostle Paul spent his emotional energy weeping over the lost (Rom. 9:2). There is no evidence that he wasted his tears on imaginary persons or their fictional grief. Erasing the line that reality draws between what's real and what isn't real radically changes our ability to communicate the critical need to appropriately respond to biblical content and spiritual truth.

Entertainment, indeed, may elicit a variety of responses but has no authority from God, as preaching does, to mandate moral action in response to its content. The TV viewer, therefore, responds in ways appropriate for drama. Sympathetic involvement in the struggles of the main character, for example, can evoke laughing, crying, or any number of emotional responses. These responses differ markedly, however, from responses to preaching. While it is no sin to ignore entertainment, preaching is a divinely appointed vehicle for conveying truth that carries with it necessary moral obligations on the part of its hearers. James 4:17 tells us, "Therefore to him that knoweth to do good, and doeth it not, to him it is sin." Not responding to truth is sin. Such moral obligations involve consequences. In Luke 13:3 Jesus said, ". . . except ye repent, ye shall all likewise perish." Seldom does a viewer's response to the content of a TV program become a necessary moral obligation.

After watching a nuclear disaster destroy life as we know it, what does the typical TV viewer do with all his pent up urges and unspent emotions? He yawns, walks to the kitchen, opens the refrigerator, pulls out a snack, and eats it. Hardly the response one would expect if nuclear war had begun in earnest. It shares no link with the content of the communication. Neither is it required. He could just as easily go to bed, to work, or to the gym. Where is the necessary connection between eating a sandwich and the end of the world? Viewer response is both optional and trivial. The viewer may be moved emotionally, but no response other than that was intended, hence the whole experience is trivialized. This passive, artificial link between TV content and response—this dissonance between data content and viewer response—spills over and contaminates listener response to preaching.

Effective preaching must maintain a rational consistency between its content and its listeners' responses. Preaching seeks responses that are *necessary* because God's Word *requires* them. Preaching seeks responses that are neither arbitrary, optional, nor inappropriate but are in accord with its content. Preaching tells its listeners *why* as well as *what* God requires. With preaching there is a necessary link connecting preaching data to listener response, and that link is the authority of the Word of God. The *desire* of the obedient listener to follow the authority of God's Word seals this connection.

Selective Passivity
To maintain that TV conditions viewers toward passivity, on the one hand, while admitting it motivates millions

of people to spend billions of dollars on goods and services on the other hand sounds like a contradiction. But it isn't. How then is TV's influence both passive and active?

Two major factors influence viewers toward a kind of selective passivity. First of all, TV rarely calls for something other than a commercial response. Certainly it does shape us in complex ways, yet far and away this commercial goal is most frequently realized. By the time Americans reach the age of forty they have seen more than 250,000 TV commercials, all having the same objective—get the consumer to buy.

From cars to golf clubs, TV excels at motivating us to acquire tangible things. On TV even the intangible becomes concrete—life insurance turns into a rock. Allowing for exceptions such as the occasional altruistic program on breast cancer prompting women to get mammograms the

> "America pays its heftiest salaries to those who make us forget our responsibilities. Responsibility is not amusing."

next day or the public service bulletin board announcing upcoming community events, TV solicits responses associated with monetary motives. It does not reinforce the reality of unseen spiritual concepts. By design TV teaches us to subjugate the invisible realm of the spiritual to the tangible acquisition of the possessions of the material world. And thus we become even more sensitized to images and calloused toward the abstract.

In contrast to TV themes, preaching primarily, though not exclusively, concerns itself with the intangible, the invisible, and the nonmonetary. Forgiveness, righteousness, and holiness are abstract concepts. The whole counsel of God covers change of character, conformity to Christ, the glory of God. These intangible themes define the very heart of preaching.

Preaching must present the invisible as real and the tangible as temporal and transitory. Christ, the Holy Spirit, salvation, heaven, hell, judgment, Satan, and angels are real, while cars, houses, and weedeaters are transitory. Paul clearly states this paradox in 2 Corinthians 4:16, "for the

> "This is the Sunday morning hurdle that effective preaching must jump over—preaching to programmed people who have been captured, conditioned, saturated, and changed. Sadly, many of us never jump this hurdle but crash into it and fall."

things which are seen are temporal; but the things which are not seen are eternal."

Accordingly, preaching seeks a different response than the commercial pitch from TV. To buy something is measurable. Other than attendance and offering, a visible or measurable response to preaching is somewhat limited. What is the measurable response to the holiness of God or to the changes that preaching creates during the week at home or on the job?

Secondly, the nature of entertainment seems to require freedom from the responsibility to respond. The lion's share of TV is amusement. As the talk shows, basketball games, sitcoms, football games, soaps, baseball games, dramatic series, the Olympics, or even the occasional art and nature programs indicate, we crave entertainment. America pays its heftiest salaries to those who make us forget our responsibilities. Responsibility is not amusing.

Response to preaching, however, unavoidably involves responsibility. How could it be otherwise? Scripture is replete with commands entailing human obligation.

The Sunday Morning Hurdle

The crux of the problem is that our hearers expect to experience preaching as if it were the no obligations, no responsibilities world of TV, and this expectation is invalid. Benefiting from preaching will never include the ease, entertainment, and effortless experience of TV. At no time should we expect the job of the listener to synchronize with the ease of the viewer. When the form changes, so must the role. To benefit from preaching, listeners must adjust their expectations to meet new obligations and adapt their roles as listeners in accord with the new requirements. In other words, they must make the transition from watching, feeling, and remaining passive to hearing, thinking, and responding in biblical ways.

It is counterproductive for preaching to ignore this distinction and treat preaching like TV for one is fish, the other foul. This mixed up approach creates a strange role reversal where such persons want to watch the preacher instead of listen to him, to feel the message instead of think about it, and to remain passive rather than respond and act. The results are roughly equivalent to handing out ear plugs and blindfolds. Preaching requires something more and something different. With preaching, hearers must first give, only then can they receive. Attention, concentration, and the effort to think the preacher's thoughts along with him are all necessary to "get anything out of" a spoken message. TV offers the role of full-time taker, a one way street. Like an iron lung that breathes for you, it supplies every need without input. No wonder so many people sitting in church moan over not being fed—they are expecting to receive without giving first. This appalling situation prevails in churches everywhere.

Using verbal means and in life changing ways, we must preach to those who are conditioned to visual, entertainment-saturated communication. We must improve our preaching both to overcome the obviously negative effects of poor preaching and to meet this new media challenge. This is the Sunday morning hurdle that effective preaching must jump over—preaching to programmed people who have been captured, conditioned, saturated, and changed. Sadly, many of us never jump this hurdle but crash into it and fall. We need to leap over the barriers that hours and days of TV watching have mounted up in our way.

Comparison of TV and Preaching		
Roles:	Viewer	Listener
Form:	Images	Words
Pathway:	Eyes	Ears
Target:	Right Brain	Left Brain
Setting:	Casual	Formal

CHAPTER FOUR

Seven New Kinds of Listeners

Most preachers are familiar with some version of the sermon evaluation form. Standard forms include the introduction, main points, conclusion, context, illustrations, exegesis, and content. Using such measuring sticks, seminary teachers can assign grades to aspiring homeliticians.

Although "Television Tom" has never seen the evaluation form from your old homiletics class, he has his own. And while it doesn't resemble yours or probably any seminary version, it's nonetheless

> "Far too often we grade ourselves on the curve when by his scale we have flunked the course."

operational. While you preach, he checks your performance against the categories important to him—"Am I interested in the topic?" or "What will this do for me?" He totals your score then decides whether he'll return next Sunday.

To identify the contents of the evaluation form in the mind of "Television Tom," to know by what criteria he rates the preacher and his message, and to understand what controls and conditions his responses to your preaching is absolutely crucial. Far too often we grade ourselves on the curve when by his scale we have flunked the course. We have assumptions about our listeners that are no longer true. TV has changed them. So the key question is: What does Television Tom's sermon evaluation form look like?

To answer this question we need only make the following assumption: he patterns it after that most comfortable and accustomed form of communication—TV. In short, he compares what he wants from preaching to what he gets from TV.

Our hearers, our Television Toms, are *conditional listeners*. Meet their conditions by giving them what they want and they'll listen. But when you don't, they tune you out.

The "Big Seven" Conditions for Listening
People watch thousands of hours of TV because they "get something" out of it.[1] But what?

Week after week, year in and year out, viewers consume TV because they receive back from TV of one or more of the "Big Seven." In order of importance they are:

- entertainment
- relaxation
- baby-sitting
- escape from loneliness
- information
- escape from reality and responsibility
- relief from boredom[2]

The desire to get or to fix these commodities, or a combination of them, covers over 90 percent of what keeps people hooked on TV.

When people come to church, even if they could, they don't automatically lay these desires aside for these same motives are operating, consciously or unconsciously, when they sit down in front of you on Sunday morning. Church architecture, organ music, and a bulletin don't change them.

Furthermore, like the unwelcome side effects of an experimental drug, the Big Seven have produced individuals who conform to one or more of the following seven kinds of listeners. Obviously, these categories attempt to define, but can't exhaust, TV's influence on our hearers' expectations, but when the Television Toms in your audience assign grades, they use the following decision-criteria for a sermon's worth. The following TV temperaments describe various personality types of programmed people and how they're likely to score your preaching.

The Feelings-Oriented Listener: Soapy Sylvia

A person who consumes TV out of loneliness, boredom, or to escape reality is a prime candidate for becoming a feelings-oriented listener. Let's call her "Soapy Sylvia." Often straving for emotional stimulation or relief from the general miseries of life, she finds in TV's soaps and sitcoms the emotional "back-rub" she seeks.[3] Sylvia loves TV as one friend loves another. When it breaks, she takes it to the hospital. Singles, widows, the elderly, retired and divorced persons often fit here. With an abundance of discretionary time and comparatively few responsibilities, they seek a surrogate "TV family" and the emotional support that it provides. Examples of this type of programming are listed in *TV Guide* as "the shows that will make you feel better."[4]

The feelings-oriented listener evaluates the worth of the sermon by the impact of the emotional charge it carries. It's the voltage that counts. Sometimes with little regard for truth, Soapy Sylvia gives the highest grades for hype, energy, and feelings of exhilaration, inspiration, and stimulation. Frequently, she equates the Holy Spirit's ministry with taking an emotional bath during the sermon. Since content takes a back seat to mood, a successful sermon is one that generates a powerful internal emotional environment. When disappointed, the feelings-oriented listener says, "His preaching doesn't move me," or "I don't feel anything when he preaches." Despite hearing the truth, she doesn't feel she has received a blessing unless she leaves with a feeling. Warm fuzzy sensations go over best.

The Entertainment-Oriented Listener:
Gameshow Gary

Closely akin to feelings-oriented Soapy Sylvia, yet possessing distinctly different characteristics, is Gameshow Gary, the entertainment-oriented listener. To relax after work or to enjoy a legitimate movie because we like to be entertained, nearly all of us who watch TV fall to a greater or lesser extent into this category with Gary.

> "Deciding on the worth of a sermon based on whether or not it was clever, exciting, or funny weighs preaching in TV's balances. Yet Gary and millions of his friends grade preaching this way."

Trouble comes, however, when Gary begins to evaluate preaching by entertainment's standards. According to Jay Leno, entertainment's crown prince, entertainment should not make social, moral, political, or profound statements.[5] It just temporarily lightens the load then leaves off where it began. Even Ecclesiastes 2:2 tells us, "I said of laughter, It is mad: and of mirth, What doeth it?" Deciding on the worth of a sermon based on whether or not it was clever, exciting, or funny weighs preaching in TV's balances. Yet Gary and millions of his friends grade preaching this way.

Preaching is not entertainment, although at times it may be entertaining. Even profound content is wasted on the heedless, so gaining and maintaining Gameshow Gary's interest and attention is prerequisite to his comprehension. Preaching that doesn't impart understanding has missed its objective, and sleeping parishioners make any preacher look bad. Humor proves a useful tool if used conscientiously, not as an end in itself, as in the entertainment world, but as a means of helping Gameshow Gary understand truth.

Preachers of the Word must speak out about the profound and critical issues of life which elevate, transform, and change even those, like Gary, who will not or cannot listen without first being entertained.[6]

The Consumer Mentality:
Shipping Network Nellie

Entire batteries of neurologists, psychologists, psychiatrists, attorneys, medical doctors, and sundry other professionals in marketing, advertising, and communications marshal their creative forces to give birth to just one TV commercial.[7] But such ridiculous sums of money—thirty to forty billion dollars a year—are justifiable to their sponsors only if the resulting sales equal the initial outlay. Little danger exists in overstating the control of commercials over our consummate consumer's—Shopping Network Nellie's—attitudes, values, and behavior, since she exposes her mind, will, and pocketbook to such Herculean powers hundreds of times every week. In Mastering Contemporary Preaching, Bill Hybels remarks,

> Unchurched people today are the ultimate consumers. We may not like it, but for every sermon we preach, they're asking, Am I interested in that subject or not? If they aren't, it doesn't matter how effective our delivery is: theirminds will check out.[8]

As a result, Nellie's attitudinal stance toward preaching is, "I am waiting for you to show me the benefits of your product. Make me want to listen. Create in me a demand." Preachers can no longer count on a hearing for the Word of God based on its authority alone even in the church. The consumer mentality hungers to know, "What will your product do for me?"

Without question the Bible is both authoritative and relevant, but consumer-listeners demand proof. When preachers capitalize on this need for proof, they provide their hearers with a powerful reason to listen. This is not to say that preachers should become salesmen first, yet this need for proof necessitates setting forth the Gospel's advantages as well as its obligations.

The Fantasy Thinker: Daydreamin' Dave

By the touch of an easily controlled button, people who watch television to escape the pain of present problems or to avoid unpleasant responsibilities transport themselves into Hollywood's painless world of TV fantasy.[9] Let's call our viewer Daydreamin' Dave. After dozens of hours spent each week detached from the real world, Dave sits down in the pew on Sunday morning to hear you preach. Application of truth to real life jars Dave and forces him to think on those unpleasant issues he neatly avoided all week long through his escape hatch called TV. His mind strays in and out of the message as he seeks a pleasanter alternative; he is like a lost child in a department store wandering aimlessly up and down the aisles.

Whether or not Ross Perot watches TV, he is the richest, if not the most famous, of all the new breed of fantasy thinkers. As reported by *USA Today,* when asked how he got his idea for EDS, his multi-billion dollar company, he replied, "I was daydreaming in church during a sermon."[10] Of course daydreaming during sermons is nothing new, yet TV helps to aggravate, if not also generate, the scope and the intensity of this debilitating practice.

In lieu of using the preacher's message as a road map, Daydreamin' Dave uses it instead as a "spring-board" pro-pelling him into a world of his own.[11] When his mind is so affected, his failure to track along with the words of the message weakens its meaning and erodes its impact. Thus, making the transition from objective truth to real life for Dave is both unfamiliar and unwelcome territory, since reality on Sunday and fantasy during the week clash.

While TV gives Sylvia, Gary, Nellie, and Dave what they want in terms of fun and feelings, at the same time it stores millions of unforgettable images in their minds and teaches them certain prime directives of the media mentality. Consequently, the next three listeners characterize certain side effects of TV consumption. The first "side effect" from TV that listeners experience in church is how they perceive and evaluate the appearance of the preacher.

The Visually Oriented Listener: Eyeball Annie

Eyeball Annie tends to equate form with function. In other words her motto is: a thing is as a thing appears. For Annie and her visually oriented friends, the visual form matters first and most, as McLuhan said, "The medium is the message." Warren Wiersbe notes,

[W]hatever we learn from television, we learn primarily from seeing and not from hearing. This distinction is important, because the emphasis in the Bible is on hearing and not on seeing. "So then faith comes by hearing, and hearing by the word of God" (Rom. 10:17). Television has helped to create a society of watchers, not listeners, people who are fascinated by pictures, not educated by words.[12]

> "Not that listeners place greater weight on your clothing, facial expressions, gestures, and church furniture than on sermon content, but rather that the message which these visual images send becomes the grid through which they interpret the content."

For example, signs in department stores often display these words, "as advertised on TV." When the customer can feel, see, handle, and smell the product if he wishes, why does it matter if it was advertised on TV?

It matters to advertisers for two reasons. They know that because content rides piggyback on form, TV imparts its credibility to the thing advertised. TV can legitimize anything. Secondly, research suggests that when a potential buyer sees the print on the sign, the visual image stored in his mind's eye will tend to be recalled. An association is made between the image and the print which reinforces demand for the item. Bingo! He buys!

This phenomenon is known as *evoked recall* and it works. What has happened? A mere visual form has authorized reality. From presidential candidates to car manufacturers, visual images preside over all. In our culture, image is gospel. How many items in your home did you first see on TV? Of what significance is this to preachers?

When nonchurched people like Eyeball Annie apply this principle of evoked recall to real ministers, a nightmare springs to life. During the preaching service, evoked recall goes to work. This means the real minister gets evaluated in terms of his media counterpart. Annie makes a comparison and renders a verdict. Does the reality that TV depicts preachers as either wimps, crooks, or perverts sway that verdict? Evoked recall says it does. Visual listeners appraise what they hear (content) by what they see (form). The imaginary interprets the reality.

Preachers must value this knowledge. Not that listeners place greater weight on your clothing, facial expressions, gestures, and church furniture than on sermon content, but rather that the message which these visual images send becomes the grid through which they interpret the content. When they can't relate to the form, they tend to reject the content; when form and content are at odds, they tend to side with form.

Can a goofy looking preacher proclaim a credible message? Not to the Eyeball Annies and Optical Olivias. Pay attention to your appearance. What message does it preach? Find out in your culture what message your visual image projects—talk to your wife, church leaders, or trusted friends. Their input enhances your image.

The Passive Nonresponder: Inert Eddie

We have shown that TV disciples its viewers in a kind of selective passivity.[13] Through media, Inert Eddie can escape the drudgery of everyday life, enjoy emotional stimulation, be released from boredom, or find companionship entirely within an imaginary environment divorced from responsibility, accountability, or the need to respond. TV severs the information-response umbilical cord.[14] Eddie enjoys this freedom until he finds himself in church where a man up front says God expects change. In church Eddie hears Scripture such as James 4:17, "To him who knows to do good, and doesn't do it, to him it is sin." Inert Eddie suddenly realizes God expects him to respond to the truth. In preaching, the information-response umbilical cord reattaches.

"Why so little change in my listeners?" may be the biggest, thorniest, most discouraging question pastors face in preaching. The connection between TV and passivity receives a lion's share of the blame. Those who imbibe TV must realize it makes them inert. We can't expect people who have logged dozens of hours in their TV-induced environment of passivity during the week to suddenly snap out of it and start actively responding on Sunday. It's out of character. A huge gap exists between the number of hours Inert Eddie logs in front of the TV with no required response and the relatively few hours he spends in church where he is called to action.

On an average, families watch just under thirty hours of TV each week. Assuming your people attend all three preaching services each week (a generous assumption), Sunday morning plus Wednesday and Sunday evening totals approximately three hours. The TV to preaching ratio is roughly ten to one (10:1) or thirty to three (30:3). This helps explain how TV conditions hearers toward nonresponse. It provides viewers with mountains of information disassociated from duty of any kind. TV offers high quantities of carefree information, while preaching dumps a comparatively little cargo of duty-laden content. Inert Eddie and his friends arrive at the preaching event with this defective expectation—lots of data and little duty.

The Attention-Deficit Adult: Inattentive Alice

By fueling the shift from a word-centered to an image-centered society, TV has permanently altered the attention span of the American public for spoken discourse.

Os Guiness, in his book *No God But God*, cites "the rise of the short attention span discourse (promoted by television's incredibly shrinking sound bite)."[15] The length of TV commercials is precisely geared to the typical twenty to thirty seconds attention span recent studies have measured. Historically, this is a quantum leap downward from just one hundred years ago when throngs would stand in rain or sunshine for six to eight hours to hear content-rich discourses such as during the Lincoln and Douglas debates.[16]

From among the numerous factors hindering the willingness and ability of Inattentive Alice to focus her attention on preaching, let's consider four.

Grazing—"Channel Surfing"

"Grazing" is the first. At home and at ease in her favorite chair after work with a little black box studded with control buttons in her hand, hundreds of times each evening Inattentive Alice glances and switches. When she can't process the volume of information or if it doesn't relate to her needs, hurts, or interests or just out of curiosity or boredom or just because she feels like it or for no reason at all, she surfs from channel to channel. Why are the megacorporations of America more afraid of that little black box than nuclear war? Because it poses the greater threat. They stand in awe since they realize that unless a message arrests the attention, it will never subdue a person's will or motivate a person to action. No thinking preacher can afford to take a cavalier approach to the remote control. It manipulates the attention of American adults. Never let yourself forget that during your preaching, people still graze, flip, and switch.

If it were possible to make tape recordings of listener thoughts in response to preaching, and if pastors could read and evaluate them, it would be interesting to postulate what they might reveal. Perhaps the following dialogue approximates what goes on in the thought sequence of your listeners as you preach.

> Ok here we go, the beginning of another sermon . . . as if I needed to hear more of what I'm not doing right anyway . . . I could be watching the sports reviews right now on channel 4. Ok. I'm here so I'll listen . . . I am a Christian . . . after all this is Sunday and Pastor is preaching so . . . what am I getting from this??? I don't see anything this sermon will do for me . . . O well, I'll keep on . . . maybe something will turn up, but if I were at home, I'd check another channel or two . . . just to see other options . . . something really interesting, really exciting or funny or . . . Boy, just wish I could stretch out in my easy chair and zzzzzzzzzzz . . . Pastor's illustration reminds me of that old hammock we used to have out in the backyard stretched between those two big maple trees, man, I had some great naps in that old hammock . . . O what, what did he just say???

A channel surfer is not a listener.

The Jarring Effect

Secondly, we have the "jarring effect" or more accurately labeled the "motion mechanism." This effect involves the technical interaction between the eye and the TV set. While viewing TV, the eyeball actually stays in a state of relative immobility as compared to normal every day activity. Someone may say, "That is physically impossible, the eye is actually moving rapidly from area to area." This

> ## "Imagine a TV set with one scene that didn't change— that's preaching."

widely held presumption is erroneous. The eyes move less while watching TV than in any other experience of daily life. In his book, *Four Arguments for the Elimination of TV*, Jerry Mander cites evidence from various research then concludes:

> While you are watching TV, in addition to the non-movement of the eyeball, there is a parallel freezing of the focusing mechanism. The eye remains at a fixed distance from the object observed for a longer period of time than in any other human experience. . . . [W]hile you are watching TV, no matter what is happening on the screen, the set itself remains at a fixed distance and requires only an infinitesimal change in focus.[17]

Relative to the TV screen, the distance between the eye and the picture tube remains nearly constant. This fixation amounts to staring. Watching TV, then, is staring for hours at a very bright light often in an artificially darkened environment. In this fixated state TV can maintain the interest and attention of its viewers only because of the rapid sequencing of the images across the screen. We watch what moves; that's human nature. In other words, viewer attentiveness is largely conditioned upon the mechanism of motion. A TV set, however, is a stationary object that merely displays scenes in motion. How long would viewers watch if the scene didn't move?—a very short time indeed. Imagine a TV set with one scene that didn't change—that's preaching.

TV viewers expect moving communication. Immobile preachers give their listeners nothing to watch. This lack of motion creates a jarring effect in persons like Inattentive Alice who have learned to pay attention to things that move. Immobile objects don't command attention. One pastor in the habit of writing out his sermons longhand and reading the manuscript from a woodenlike stance in the pulpit field tested this principle. Reading his manuscript but walking to and fro on the platform resulted in a dramatic rise in the attentiveness of his entire congregation.

Inattentiveness

There is a third factor influencing Inattentive Alice. Researchers have measured the response of the brain in subjects watching TV in terms of the alpha and beta waves which gauge the increase and decrease of brainwave activity. The mental state most commonly associated with meditation and ordinarily distinguished by lack of eye movement, fixation, lack of definition, idleness, inactivity, and over all body inertness is alpha sequencing. "Spaced out" characterizes this state. TV habituates our hearers into patterns of passive alpha sequencing. Perhaps that's why babysitters choose TV for their children more than anything else, for in effect they become little "space cadets."

Not always but often, TV puts people to sleep. Certainly there are various reasons unconnected to TV that people space out in church. Schedules play a part. Many people are so busy in weekly activities that anywhere they sit still for twenty minutes their bodies slowdown, and they nod off. The elderly can nap anywhere. Then, of course, ineffective preaching tends to send all of us to dreamland. In addition, when room temperatures are too warm, it's just like tossing a warm blanket over the whole congregation.

Although the causal connection between TV zombies like Inattentive Alice and inattentiveness to preaching may not be bulletproof, those who for dozens of hours each week form habits of sitting down, staring at the set, and then falling asleep can't totally shake this same three-part sequence when they sit down in church, stare at an immobile preacher, and attempt to listen.

Decontextualization

A fourth factor powerfully at work in the attention deficit adult is decontextualization. In the course of an evening's TV experience these very words, or words to this effect, are repeated like media mantras, "And now this . . . ." What do these words really mean?

Essentially these words mean that what comes after bears no connection with what has gone before. Everything stands on its own two, unrelated feet in a world where each new frame bears no necessary or discernable relationship to the others. In other words, nothing has a context. Obedient disciples learn not to associate related facts because facts are not related. Instead, TV disciplines our minds to disassociate them. Such disconnected programming can interlace unrelated topics—changing from dog food to feminine hygiene, from tablesaws to Caribbean cruises—in the course of one commercial break and then return to yet an entirely different storyline requiring orderly, contextualized thinking. The only way to make sense of these patterns is to recognize them as nonsense.

Imagine how odd it must seem when an expository preacher says, "Now in this context we see . . ." or explains in a passage what goes before and comes after, who speaks and who is spoken to. "In the context"—what context? Fitting together associated facts is possible only for people who can listen and think contextually. TV teaches decontextualized habits which move us away from the contextual mindset needed to gain understanding from preaching that respects the scriptural context.

By combining these four forces, the sorry portrait of all the Inattentive Annies sitting in your church emerges. Channel surfing habituates them to mindless change and leaves little time to tap their interest before it shifts away. Maintaining their attention without providing endless moving images is contrary to those passive alpha sequencing patterns developed by staring at the TV set, and carrying them through the transitions is especially precarious since deconextualization has conditioned them to disassociate related facts.

Comparison of TV and Preaching		
Roles:	Watching	Listening
Analysis:	Feeling	Thinking
Response:	Passivity	Action

CHAPTER FIVE

The TV Pulpit and the Electronic Pew

In the early 1950s Bishop Fulton J. Sheen, a Roman Catholic priest, presented Life Is Worth Living, the first televised preaching program in America. Today, both Christian and secular stations offer a variety of church services via satellite, cable networks, and regular TV. This new electronic church and its media preachers have mushroomed into a multibillion dollar industry that now reaches viewers around the world and whose impact cannot be ignored.

Reckoning with the impact of the electronic church on the individuals in the pew falls heavily on the shoulders of the local pastor. Right or wrong, what media preachers do on TV does have an impact on the average preacher on Sunday morning when he stands behind his pulpit. The fallout from the scandals of the televangelists and others has changed how people in and out of the church view the messenger and his message. But how? What are the effects of televised preaching upon preaching in the local church? In what ways has it changed the average pastor's task on Sunday morning? The answers to these questions will help pastors understand the impact of televised preaching on their congregations.

Understanding Televised Preaching: What It Isn't and What It Is

Watching TV is not discipleship.
Discipleship is more than facts and knowledge. Becoming a disciple involves molding character and conduct. TV lacks certain essentials that discipleship requires, and the most vital of these is the personal dimension. In Luke 6:40 Jesus said,

> The disciple is not above his master: but every one that is perfect shall be as his master.

In *No God But God* Os Guiness uses the term *modernity* to remark about the negative forces of modern technology (of which TV is a stellar component) upon the church when he says,

> "Modernity simultaneously makes **evangelism** infinitely easier and **discipleship** infinitely harder."[1]

TV may present the life-changing Gospel but can't follow it up for lack of the personal dimension. The following seven facts support this claim.

1. The fifty-eight personal "one another" ministries of the New Testament are logistically impossible over the air—for example, to forgive one another, to be patient with one another, or to serve one another. Long distance discipling is not the Lord's plan.
2. Flesh and blood models (Luke 6:40) are either absent or have been replaced by the preacher as a celebrity rather than as a servant.
3. Personal communication and accountability don't exist. The care and discipline of the local church,

baptism, and the Lord's Supper are all essentials for
the true disciple.

4. Personalized prayer is impossible—to learn specific
   requests takes time and person to person contact.
5. Revelation 3–4 requires individual diagnosis of the
   congregation and its needs *before* prescription, not
   generic but personally-tailored messages designed
   by the pastor to meet the specific needs of the
   congregation at a particular time.
6. The gifts of the church that benefit the body—the
   warmth, love, care, true fellowship, forgiveness,
   and support both financial and emotional—are
   absent.
7. TV lacks the indwelling of the Holy Spirit to
   empower the discipler for his or her ministry.
   Although it is certain that the Spirit of God has
   moved people to kneel in front of their TV sets and
   receive Christ as Savior, that's evangelism, not discipleship. Jesus did not say, "Just get decisions," He
   said, "Make disciples." Discipleship includes personal follow up, teaching, and support of this new
   believer. The Great Commission mandates "Teach
   them to observe all things whatsoever I have com-
   manded you" (Matt. 28:20). This essential ministry
   requires a Spirit-filled person. An image of a preacher is an image, not a person. That's why, as Os
   Guiness claims, TV preaching makes evangelism easier while at the same time it is making discipleship
   harder.[2] Those electronic images of the media
   church don't constitute the reality. Never has a TV
   been indwelt by the Spirit of God like a genuine
   Spirit-filled, truth-imparting Christian.

Watching TV is not true worship.

Under the false assumption that they are worshiping God,
many sincere yet mistaken people choose to stay home
on Sundays rather that assemble in a church. They believe
that watching a church service on TV qualifies as genuine
worship. God prescribes the conditions of true worship,
however, and failure to meet these qualifications means
failure to worship. TV fails to offer genuine worship; it
offers an artificial alternative.

In his book, *The Integrity Crisis,* Warren Weirsbe provides
a key insight about worship:

> True ministry implies involvement: we're worshiping in
> the holy presence of God, and we're obligated to hear God's
> Word and obey it. When we put religion on TV, a subtle
> force goes to work that transforms everything. *The viewer
> does not attend the same service as the people in the
> sanctuary or in the TV studio.* The people in the congregation
> can be participants: the viewer at home is a spectator. The
> congregation is a living corporate fellowship, assembled for
> worship; the viewer is a solitary watcher, even if he's not
> alone. Religion on TV is not the same as religion in person.
> It's a new kind of religion altogether."[3]

The same logic that considers watching worship to be
even roughly the same thing as true worship must also
reason that watching murder means the same thing as
participating in murder. But spectator-viewers aren't
participators, and viewing a worship service on TV places
the would-be worshiper in the role of spectator.

Worship "in Spirit"

In Scripture God sets down two clear conditions for
genuine worship. In John chapter 4 Jesus explained these
conditions to the woman at the well. "*God is a Spirit*; and
they that worship Him must worship Him **in spirit** and **in
truth**" (4:24). "In Spirit" worship requires the presence
and blessing of the Holy Spirit. By using the term
"indwelling," theologians speak of His presence in two
related but different ways. One is individual indwelling,
"the Spirit of God dwells in you," (Rom. 8:9)—individually
the Spirit resides within every genuine believer. The second
is the collective indwelling of the Spirit within the entire
corporate body of the church when it assembles as in
1 Corinthians 3:16–17, (dative plural) and (nominative
plural). This indwelling refers to the church as an
assembled group.

The Christian who stays home on Sunday morning and
"goes to church in his living room" via TV may have the
first but not the second kind of indwelling—individual
indwelling but not corporate.

To the early church (Acts 20:7) and to believers today who assemble on Sunday (Heb. 10:25) God's promise states, "Wherever two or three are **gathered together in My Name** there will I be in their midst" (Matt. 18:20). This requires the second collective sense. Isolated individuals viewing TV cannot fulfill this biblical requirement and therefore don't enjoy its benefits.

This presence of Christ through the Spirit has special importance for preaching, because preaching involves more than just the preacher, it extends to the congregation also. In *The Sacred Anointing*, Tony Sargent quotes D. Martin Lloyd-Jones:

> The very presence of a body of people in itself is a part of the preaching. . . . It is not a mere gathering of people; Christ is present. This is the great mystery of the Church. There is something in the very atmosphere of *Christian people meeting together* to worship God and to listen to the preaching of the Gospel.[4]

Televised preaching fails to duplicate this mystery. Sargent has written at great length about the Holy Spirit's ministry of "unction" in preaching. He rightly contends that preaching is more than the cold, calculated transference of information in the form of words. It requires a supernatural component that only the Holy Spirit of God can supply, and this He does in a fashion not subject to air waves or electrons. TV can't capture the Spirit's unction like a genie in a bottle and then let Him out when the tape plays. This unction of the Spirit, however, is nonetheless real and actually vital to the preacher in his task. In fact, preaching without the aid and blessing of the sovereign work of the Spirit fails to qualify as preaching at all. TV could never bottle and sell "unction"; it can only record it.

> "Through a strange sort of media-induced paradox, televised preaching can evangelize but not disciple, edify the individual worshiper but not become corporate worship for the church body."

Worship "in Truth"

What about the second condition for true worship—
"in truth"? Truth was fashioned and given in words as
the divinely chosen form, "Thy word is truth" (John17:17).
Through words, God has chosen a form of communication
not only superior to images but also consistent with His
invisible character. Whether graven or electronic, images
are ill-suited and inappropriate means of worship for an
intangible God. True, an image of a word is still a word, yet
worship that replaces words with images, as TV does,
effectively ignores the invisible character of God.

> "And the LORD spake unto you out of the midst of the
> fire: ye heard the voice of the words, but saw no similitude
> (image); only ye heard a voice. And he declared unto you
> his covenant, which he commanded you to perform, even
> ten commandments; and he wrote them upon two tables of
> stone." (Deut. 4:12–13).

God was long at issue with Israel over sensuous, image-
oriented worship. In this passage and others, He places
images over against words as opposing forms of worship.
In Spirit and in Truth worship is mediated by the Spirit
of God through the instrumentality of His Word, not images.
If TV doesn't qualify for authentic worship, into what
category must it fit?

What TV Preaching Is

Televised preaching and Christian programming provide
a variety of substantial benefits for viewers. Gospel singing
groups and related ministries offer entertainment of a
Christian sort. Through TV, Christian education blesses the
lives of thousands of believers each year, supplying useful
facts and making available a variety of products and services.
At times it stimulates them to useful action in their churches
and communities. In this regard it serves as an information
service—an "electronic bulletin board."

Through televised evangelistic crusades, many
unbelievers come to Christ each year. In its evangelistic
role, TV functions like an "electronic gospel tract," nothing
more. It's radio with pictures, like voice mail where you
see and hear the sender.

Through a strange sort of media-induced paradox, televised preaching can evangelize but not disciple, edify the individual worshiper but not become corporate worship for the church body.

How Authentic Preaching Differs from TV Preaching

Authentic preaching has authority and purpose.

Biblically and theologically considered, authentic preaching differs from televised preaching in authority and purpose. Authentic preaching calls for unique authority.

> Preach the word; be instant in season, out of season; reprove, rebuke, exhort with all longsuffering and doctrine. For the time will come when they will not endure sound doctrine; but after their own lusts shall they heap to themselves teachers, having itching ears" (2 Tim. 4:2–3).

Those who would preach to the church must be examined, ordained, and commissioned by a church if their preaching is to be authoritative in the church. In addition, to preach with authority to an individual local church should require some type of special recognition or official call from that church. Even when invited to speak, the authority of a visiting evangelist or fellow preacher is not equivalent to that of the office-bearing pastor of the church. How then can uninvited preachers be authoritative? Airwaves can't grant authority.

"Without character there is no biblical authority."

What's the point of those long lists of qualifications in 1 Timothy 3:1–13 and in Titus 1:6–9 detailing God's standards for preachers if anyone with enough money and influence can fail those requirements and still preach with authority? These passages mandate that Christlike character be exemplified in those who proclaim the Gospel. Without character there is no biblical authority. God says character is at the heart of the issue for preachers, but not unexamined or only self-examined character. Authority to preach is reserved for those who exemplify Christlikeness and pass examination by those who are supposed to know the life

and related behavioral issues of the candidate well enough
to determine whether or not he qualifies. Who examines
and certifies the integrity of the preacher? The church does.
How much can the average TV viewer know about a stranger
on the screen?

Permitting preachers without character to influence the
church is tantamount to allowing a surgeon with a mail
order medical degree to cut open your body. Because TV
either minimizes or ignores altogether this very issue of
character, men without integrity often preach over the
air. Often the results have been ruinous. When speaking to
the church about treatment of pastors without integrity,
Paul told Timothy, "Them that sin rebuke before all, that
others also may fear" (1 Tim. 5:20). Lose your character,
and your authority to preach expires with it. When the issue
of authority as a perquisite for preaching is dismissed
and the local church's God-given role of examining and
recognizing men of character is disregarded, the lack or
complete absence of integrity in preachers can result.

To disregard these principles violates the requirements
for the installation and maintenance of preachers required
by the Pastoral Epistles in 1 Timothy 3:1–13 and Titus 1:6–9.
All this would be uncalled for if authority were not an issue.

Today's answer to Paul's rhetorical question in Romans
10:15, "And how shall they preach, except they be sent?"
in some cases would be, "Go on TV." Although preaching
cannot be divorced from this issue of being sent, televised
preaching often attempts to do an end run around it.
Authority is inconsequential and irrelevant on TV. It
disregards spiritual authority in preaching and operates
instead upon the false presumption that all preaching by
anyone, anywhere, to everyone, everywhere, is the same.
It isn't. All preaching is not equal. Embracing this media
view is alien to the New Testament.

But what about the case where an ordained and biblically
sound preacher televises sermons from his church? The
authority issue remains unchanged. He may impart truth
to the individual, he may evangelize the lost, but he can't
preach with authority to any church but his own. Anyone
attempting to prove otherwise from the New Testament will
be hard pressed indeed. The authority of the Bible remains
the same, but one pastor's authority fails to extend across

town, let alone across the country to encompass a different church. A televised pastor from a church in Indiana lacks the same authority to preach to a church in California. Preaching over the airwaves imparts only distance to the message, not authority.

Nearly every instance of preaching in the New Testament by office-bearers uses the word *khrux*—a herald or mouthpiece who qualifies as an official spokesman. Of the three notable exceptions of noncommissioned persons who preached, all were in direct disobedience to Jesus' revealed will—the leaper in Mark 1:45, the man of the Gadarenes in Mark 5:19–20, and the deaf and dumb man in Mark 7:35–37. All the results were negative. Is this what happens today when noncommissioned men pretend to preach with the authority of an office-bearing pastor?

Authentic preaching builds the church body as a whole.

Authentic preaching differs from preaching on TV in a second way. In contrast to those heralds on TV who speak primarily to individuals, biblical pastors preach with concern for the building up of the church body as a whole, a mark more encompassing and inclusive. Roles and goals of church leaders, philosophy of ministry issues, involvement in that particular community's cultural and social issues are all unique to individual churches and their specialized gifts and needs. Authentic preaching directly relates to all such matters that affect the harmony and health of the body collectively.

> The purpose of preaching, then, is to effect changes among the members of God's church that build them up individually and that build up the body as a whole. . . . Corporately, such preaching builds up the church as a body in the relation of the parts to the whole, and the whole to God and to the world . . . . Probably today there is much less emphasis on the corporate aspects of edification (the upbuilding of the entire body, as a body) than there ought to be. In America, at least, we still wade around in the foam of a mighty wave of "rugged individualism," as it has been called.[5]

TV preaching certainly appeals to this rugged

individualism for two reasons. First and most obvious is that TV preachers reach the ones and twos isolated in their living rooms; they never address the assembled church since to do so requires a personal appearance. Secondly, TV preachers cannot diagnose individual needs or specific sins that convict a particular individual, whereas biblical preaching must diagnose before it prescribes. To do otherwise is tantamount to dispensing pills at random, a kind of spiritual quackery. The knowledge necessary for meeting specialized needs of individual local churches and individual members is simply not available to TV preacher.

A Question of Impact

What influence does televised preaching have currently and what will its impact be in the future?

Figures on how many persons watch TV preachers but never darken the door of a church are inconclusive. According to a National Council of Churches/National Religious Broadcasters survey, TV preachers who claim to have ten to twenty million viewers are whistling in the dark.[6] Conservatively we can say millions, for reasons that favor the "electronic pew" are easy to find.

The overall preaching setting in churches demands more of everything from its listeners including money. Pastors must concede that listening to televised preaching is less expensive, less time consuming, and less stressful than driving to church. Furthermore, it requires no accountability to others.

The trend points to a future rise in inhabitants of the electronic pew. Envisioning the ultimate "TV church" of the future where people never leave their living rooms takes little imagination. In *A Church for the 21st Century*, Leith Anderson describes how such a church might develop.

> TV churches do not now exist as they might in the twenty-first century. But imagine a form of the church that might develop. Millions of Americans are aging into retirement. There are already more people over 65 than there are teenagers—for the first time in the country's history. Many will become shut-ins who can't or won't leave home for a church service. At the same time, the rise in crime in some sections of the country has turned homes into fortresses

with bars on the windows, gates at the doors, and electronic security systems connected to the police department. Those people don't go out any more than they have to. Some work at home via computers with modems. Many have at least their pizza, if not all their food, delivered. Why not stay home for church as well?[7]

Inevitable Comparison and Contrast

For these reasons it is difficult to conceive of televised preaching as aiding local churches. Further, local preachers experience unnerving "downward" comparisons with TV's religious spokesmen. Remarks such as, "Our preacher doesn't measure up to so-and-so when it comes to . . ." or "I like . . . better than our pastor when it comes to prophecy" are common. These evaluations may be accurate, yet the comparisons are problems. Not all preachers have the same gifts, nor did the Lord intend for each to have the same ministries; diversity is planned by God. In recognition of these differences 1 Corinthians 3:22 declares "All are yours," meaning that all God-given preachers have something to offer God's people. Yet such a point of view toward local pastors is the exception rather than the rule.

Inevitable comparisons lead to inevitable contrast. "Yesterday, Pastor So-and-So (a TV preacher) said, ' . . . '; he was so good, I just love to hear him. I wish our pastor would preach on that sometime, but he doesn't." No unselfish preacher would knowingly withhold true spiritual benefits from his people, but the timing and use of certain biblical subjects by a TV preacher can become a competing alternative to following the teaching plan of the local church pastor.

Unwittingly, perhaps, but sometimes purposely so, TV preachers present unorthodox doctrinal views and divergent theological positions. Whenever an alternative view is presented, the opportunity arises for conflict. In America, no certifying organization guards the standards for the preaching of doctrine on TV, nor should there be one. Yet sadly, fascination with the bizarre in religion is rivaled only by the parade of freaks on the latest TV talk show; it's notoriety that allures viewers not orthodoxy.[8]

In addition to certain biblical subjects, the media popularizes certain preaching styles which become yet another standard of comparison. The pastor of a church under two hundred, who wears ten or twelve different hats already and has no staff, can't compare with the sophistication, illustrations, outlines, quotes, and finesse of preaching style with a pastor of two thousand members who has a large staff and plentiful resources. Some TV preachers have passed neither an ordination exam nor a formal test of theological orthodoxy, why should they be held up as models?

Accountability for Contributions

Paradoxically, many who watch preachers on TV send their money to a preacher they've never really seen in person, they don't know, and who will never give them an accounting for their contributions because "it's such a large TV ministry." Instead, they could give their money to their local church where every penny is accounted for in a budget and where they can literally see and oversee how it is spent. A rational explanation of such irrational giving must conclude that media lends its credibility to otherwise biblically "incredible" ministries, so that thousands of people give millions of dollars to feel they're a part of something big, visible, and significant. This giving pattern constitutes a disastrous drain on local church finances as does our next comparison, the matter of giving time.

Responsible Use of Time

Since the TV is on thirty hours a week in the typical home, every hour spent watching TV inevitably lessens the hours available for individual involvement in and service to church-related ministries. We'll never know the extent of this drain on the resources of the local church to serve both the members and the larger community.

Furthermore, in the misdirected interests of "saving time," many who listen to televised preaching stay home from the local church on Sunday and tell themselves, "We've already heard one preacher this week, why make it two? Enough is enough."

The Challenge

The local church and the local pastor face an enormous challenge from TV. To meet this challenge for the time and commitment of Christians, local pastors must sharpen their preaching skills or perish.

So, let's look now at how preaching can improve by responding positively to TV's challenges. What a noticeable gain there can be for the church when the stay-at-homes convert to the local assembly!

What Should Preaching Do About TV?

Of all the technological forces that mold and shape us—computers, fiber optics, world-wide satellite networks, medical science—none exert greater control over us than TV. Even if Vladimir Zworykin who discovered TV's prototype—the iconoscope—in 1907 had won the Nobel prize for a vivid imagination, he never could have realized the awesome power of his invention.

Today our hearers live a TV-saturated existence which has changed individual people, the culture, and the environment. Today's preacher must face the reality that these changes are largely detrimental to preaching.

In an article from *Masterpiece Magazine* entitled "Now a word from our sponsor," John MacArthur comments on TV's effects upon preaching by asking the question,

> How does a Pastor with integrity deal with this problem?
> . . . We must find ways to make the truth of God known

to a generation that *not only doesn't want to hear, but may not even know how to listen.*[1]

In Part II of this book let's look at some ways to improve our preaching so that media-saturated people will be able to hear the Word of God.

CHAPTER SIX

Capitalize on TV

W here's the beef? "Plop, plop, fizz, fizz, O what a relief it is." "Just do it!" These and dozens of other familiar words, tunes, and images exist as permanent fixtures within the mental landscape of programmed people. How did they get there?

The brain resembles a camera with a new roll of film. When the shutter opens and exposes the film, an imprint is made. In a similar way, the sounds, concepts, and idioms of TV imprint the memory.

Today, because of TV, more people than ever before share the same information. When it comes to communicating quickly and with vigor to a wide range of persons, tapping these vast pools of shared knowledge virtually guarantees effectiveness. Paul used this principle in Acts 17:16–21. To pagan Athenians, the common media of the day (the places for exchanging ideas by telling or hearing some new thing) were the synagogues and marketplaces. Today, if a language or culture exists that all Americans share, it comes from TV.

The first thing preachers today can do to capitalize on this universal TV language is to use legitimate TV content to advantage. Since mass communication means shared knowledge, tapping into what's already there in the minds of our listeners offers a powerful way to connect with and drive home the truth. Entire concepts can be conveyed with impact by a simple phrase like "You got the right one, baby, uhh-huh"!

Why It Works Nearly Every Time

TV in general and commercials in particular provide material created at enormous expense by people who take great pains to sell their products. Most commercials follow the A-I-D-S formula: attention/interest/direction/sell. Such commercial content was designed from the beginning for maximum impact.

In addition, using appropriate TV material increases a hundredfold the probability that your hearers will relate to your point, more so than those illustrations and stories from long ago and far away about Lord So-and-So from England— the kind of arcane thing you'll find in many sermon illustration books. People don't relate to those stories because they're not part of their experiences. Why employ preaching material with a narrow breadth and appeal when you're able to garner a wider audience and greater appeal using content from TV? Since it's already in their heads, you're simply tapping what's already present. Also, TV content has instant recognition with most people no matter what their backgrounds, so you don't have to explain the illustration after you give it as with other source material. Even TV commercials are notable sources for sermon illustrations, quotes, and idioms.

Commercials

Regrettably, these windows on the world of materialism are a way of life not soon to pass off the screen, and many "programmed" children can sing and quote more commercial jingles than Bible verses.

For example, familiar but effective, the phrase from the American Express Card, "Don't leave home without it," has been popularized by TV for years; it's memorable, it's practical, and it works in other contexts: prayer, don't leave home without it; the Word of God, don't leave home without it; an attitude of dependence on God, don't leave home without it. No matter where or how many times I use this media idiom, someone remarks about it after the message. Why?

It isn't cute or clever, but it is quick and clear. When people recall and associate the phrase in a new way, it becomes ingrained. When preaching on the sufficiency of the Scriptures, I often say, "It's like that spaghetti sauce, 'It's in there.'" When learning how to witness for Christ, "It's in there"; solving problems with your wife, kids, or boss, "It's in there." Everything the Christian needs for life and godliness is "in there" (2 Peter 1:3). Plus a reverse association often happens. The next time they see the commercial, they remember the spiritual application.

Movies and Films

TV popularizes movies and films. *E.T.*, one of the top-selling movies of all time, is a story about a boy and a stranded space alien named E.T. Parallels abound between E.T. and Jesus Christ, between the boy's relationship with E.T. and the believer's relationship with Christ. E.T. does miracles, has supernatural powers, experiences death, burial, and resurrection, and even promises a second coming. In the meantime, though absent, he keeps a close personal relationship with the boy—so close, in fact, that when E.T. dies, the boy nearly perishes along with him. Although this may be a nice story, it's fiction.

One reason for this tale's enormous popularity is the deep longing within little children to have a friend who'll fix the broken things in life and be there when they are hurting. Only Jesus can do these things, and He is something E.T. isn't. He's real.

In using popular movies like *E.T.* for preaching illustrations, we can emphasize that Christ did real miracles, arose from the dead, through His Holy Spirit provides a close personal relationship with all His "little children," and He will come again for them.

Capitalize on individual movies and films while they're popular; their usefulness fades with their gradual loss of popularity.

Sports and Related Events

The Superbowl often holds the distinction of having the all-time highest viewership for a single event. For example, 133 million Americans watched as Michael Jackson danced his way through the '93 half time show. Any comment, illustration, story, or remark about that event had instant recognition and interest at that time, whether positive or otherwise, with 133 million people.

Sports are a terrific resource for human interest stories and motivational material. The thrill of victory and the agony of defeat is a universally powerful theme and has the additional advantage of reaching many men with whom you would otherwise have few points of contact. As an example I paraphrased this story from a news article,

> On November 23, 1984, Doug Flutie threw a forty-eight yard touchdown pass to Gerard Phelan in the last second of a late November game in a drizzly Orange Bowl. Taking the ball over three Miami defenders at the one yard line, the receiver fell back into the end zone and, among other things, gave Boston College a 47–45 victory over Miami. It forever changed the lives of the man who threw it and the man who caught it and gave college football a play that will never go away.[1]

The lasting effect of salvation in Christ, however, is so much greater. In one awesome moment He turns a loser into a winner, defining one's identity for a lifetime and for eternity. Amen.

Coming from behind, winning over impossible odds, and the power of team spirit when everyone does his part are commonly applicable truths for all ages and situations. In marriage, ministry, business relationships, or parenting such commonalities in human experience make persuasive examples and bring truth home to the hearer. "There hath no temptation taken you but such as is common to man" (1 Cor. 10:13). People readily identify with a shared experience.

The apostle Paul capitalized on sports metaphors. From the Olympic games he drew upon boxing, running, and wrestling (Eph. 6:12). In 1 Corinthians 9:24–27 (NIV) Paul utilizes the same concepts:

> Do you not know that in a race all the runners run, but only one gets the prize? Run in such a way as to get the prize. Everyone who competes in the games goes into strict training. They do it to get a crown that will not last; but

we do it to get a crown that will last forever. Therefore I do not run like a man running aimlessly; I do not fight like a man beating the air. No, I beat my body and make it my slave so that after I have preached to others, I myself will not be disqualified for the prize.

Major News Events

Major news events like inaugurations, calamities, wars, earthquakes, court trials, and deaths and suicides of prominent persons are powerful sources of illustrations. Occasional interruptions of sermon series to capitalize on contemporary media issues can heighten the interest of your current listeners and, in addition, draw the previously unmotivated into church, some for the first time. The recent bombing of the federal building in Oklahoma City has caused

> "During the Gulf War, the heavy hand of TV coverage monopolized the intellectual and emotional energy of our nation."

many people to ask why God would allow such an atrocity and has given preachers the opportunity to answer their question. When fear, anxiety, and concern run high, channel this energy into productive sermon illustrations.

A year or so ago I ran an ad in our local newspaper with this question: "Cult leader in Waco, Texas, claims to be Jesus Christ. Could he be? Find out what Scripture says!" That Sunday I preached to people I'd never seen! Were they curiosity seekers? Maybe. No, all of them didn't return the following Sunday, but all heard the Gospel of salvation through faith in Jesus Christ.

During the Gulf War, the heavy hand of TV coverage monopolized the intellectual and emotional energy of our nation. This focus on the war created an intensity and interest among listeners that provided a society-wide occasion for preachers to teach God's view of war. "Why is there suffering and death?" "Why does God allow dictators to commit atrocities?" "Is anything worth dying for?" *For a brief moment TV created a nation of motivated listeners.*

Preaching on such topics ministered to the hungry hearts and open ears of young and old alike.

River Phenix, the TV youth idol who portrayed the young Indiana Jones, died of a drug overdose. The teenagers in your congregation all knew it. They also knew about the suicide of the grung-rock star Kurt Cobain. One reference to the tragic deaths of these otherwise healthy and promising young men, who apparently had every earthly reason to live, brings more conviction about the evils of drugs than ten "ain't it awful how messed up young people are today" sermons. They knew these performers from TV; they felt their pain and identified with their struggles. TV is a tremendous resource for powerful, negative examples.

Why swim upstream? Instead of fighting the current, use it to your advantage. Moving the minds of the congregation off these pressing issues and onto your topic is arduous, upstream, unnecessary, and most likely useless. In these instances, wisdom directs us to go with the flow. Don't fight the tide of current events, use the waves to surf to shore!

A Caution

Words of caution are necessary. A need exists for discernment in sermon illustrations. Among the dozens of programs and commercials aired daily, many are unsuitable for use in sermons. For example, to tell a story from an off-color soap opera would imply it's O.K. to watch immorality on TV, something the Scriptures don't sanction. And beware of theological inaccuracies such as identifying the Holy Spirit with "the force" in the Star Wars movies and saying, "May the force be with you" as an allusion to the Holy Spirit. It is a parallel, maybe, but not an identification or substitute.

Thoughtlessly using TV content in messages can sometimes cross the line between relevance and irreverence—such as titling a message on giving, "And now a word from our Sponsor." In some areas of the country pastors can equate God with the sponsor, but not everywhere. Our goal should be to *utilize* media for instruction in righteousness, not to identify with it.

With these cautions in mind, pastors can and must avail themselves of this wide range of appealing and readily available illustration material.

CHAPTER SEVEN

TV's Achilles' Heel and Preaching's Power

Preachers should both capitalize on TV's strengths and exploit its weaknesses. As a form of communication, TV has serious flaws which the effective biblical communicator must identify and avoid.

For example, TV is an open-admission medium that can't discern if its viewers are six or sixty years old, single or married, healthy or sickly; it appreciates nothing of their struggles or heartaches, hopes or fears. To be sure, those behind the scenes in TV have a burning desire to know such things, but at best they must rely upon statistical analyses and demographic studies.

Imagine preaching blindfolded to a congregation on the other side of a high black curtain. That's TV—totally an impersonal one way presenter that can't see, hear, feel, or understand its subjects. It's neither flexible nor spontaneous in response to circumstances that change. People leave the room, fight with each other, or even die of heart attacks in front of it, and TV never knows, cares, or responds.

In short, TV is inflexible, nonadaptable, and incapable of any genuinely human fellowship, interaction, or concern. As a medium of communication, it qualifies as an electronic zombie, plain and simple.

Is this also the case with preaching? Could a similar description fairly characterize some preachers? If not, what is distinctive about preaching? What potential capabilities exist for preaching that TV does not and can never have?

Preaching Should Differentiate

In contrast to TV, preaching can discriminate between different kinds of people with different needs. Alert pastors who see, hear, and touch their listeners can be sensitive and respond to them as individuals.

> "In seminary or in Bible college we learned to exegete the Scripture, now we must learn to exegete the congregation."

Sadly, some pastors, for all they know about their people and for how little their sermon structure reflects the differing needs of their congregations, might as well be blindfolded. Like TV, they recognize no distinctions among their hearers and instead attempt to apply the same sermon to all ages and persons as if all had the same life situations, the same circumstances, and the same needs. None of TV's inflexibility should hold true in preaching.

For example, a pastor preaching from Philippians 4:19, "But my God shall supply all your need according to his riches in glory by Christ Jesus," can and should recognize that for a single mother with two small children, trusting the Lord to supply her needs bears little resemblance to the "empty nest" couple enjoying two steady incomes. And these two differ from the retired person facing surgery Monday morning. What qualifies as a major life-issue for the one weighs in as a low priority for the other. Overwhelming matters for the cancer patient are inconsequential to the young and healthy. Applying truth in a generic fashion without distinction reflects the impersonal nature of TV and will reap the same boring results.

The TV set is deemed unworthy of attention 65 percent of the time it's on.[1] Why? Its viewers see nothing relating to their hurts, needs, or interests. Preaching must give listeners something different.

At this point preaching enjoys strength where TV has weakness. Instead of requiring people do their own discriminating by sorting through the channels, pastors can discern doubts, fears, troubles, and concerns and sort through the generic to connect with the specific. In seminary or in Bible college we learned to exegete the Scripture, now we must learn to exegete the congregation. In so doing, preaching deletes the generic and connects with the specific. In TV, viewers search and hope; with preaching people can seek and find.

In this respect preaching is distinctively different and superior. To ignore or overlook this distinction neglects a useful tool that God has placed in your preaching tool box.

Preaching Can Be Uniquely Spirit-Empowered

In preaching God appoints Christlike, Spirit-filled people—not cassette tapes, VCRs, e-mail, or TV—but *people* with all their faults and flaws to communicate His message. In God's plan the Holy Spirit, "The Divine Person," aids and empowers the preacher for His work.

> Then Peter, *filled with the Holy Ghost,* said unto them, Ye rulers of the people, . . . (Acts 4:8)

> Then Saul (who also is called Paul,) *filled with the Holy Ghost,* set his eyes on him, And said, O full of all subtilty . . . (Acts 13:9–10a).

This work of the Spirit occurs within *people,* not electronic devices, flesh and blood, not plastic and steel, not even books or print for that matter. The Spirit of God doesn't fill (control) inanimate objects as He does preachers. Preaching is uniquely Spirit-empowered. Are, then, these other means of communication beyond significant use by the Spirit? Certainly not. God saves people who respond to rebroadcasts of preaching services just as He saves those reading a gospel tract or Christian book. But preaching is appointed and empowered by the Spirit in ways inanimate objects are not.

So what's the difference between a live preaching service and a copy of the identical service aired over TV and presented on the screen to viewers in their living rooms? If it's the identical message, word-for-word, how could its significance possibly be different? When viewed as a communications event, the ministry of the Holy Spirit during a rebroadcast sermon differs from authentic preaching in three ways—the messenger, the message, and the audience.

The messenger is empowered by the Holy Spirit.

The messenger, the preacher, is different. Live preaching has a personal dimension that TV lacks. The human spirit of the preacher, enabled by the Holy Spirit, interacts with the human spirits within the listeners. This may be an intangible reality, but it is nonetheless real. In Acts 17:16–17 when Paul looked upon the city of Athens and saw that it was given over to idols, the Bible says "his spirit was stirred in him," a term denoting emotional distress. The result, "therefore disputed he in the synagogue with the Jews." In Mark 10:21 we read, "Then Jesus beholding him [the rich young ruler] loved him, and said unto him, One thing thou lackest . . . ." His love motived Jesus to speak the truth to His audience. This interaction of preacher with people is as real today as it was for Jesus and Paul. Yet no human spirit within a TV program loves or becomes provoked toward its viewers such that it speaks and interacts with people in a similar way.

The message is edited by the Holy Spirit.

Secondly, this Spirit-guided interaction with the preacher and the assembled congregation produces significant editing of the message. Since the Holy Spirit often uses the emotions and thoughts of a pastor *during* his preaching, the power of the Spirit fills his sails and pushes him in a different direction than he would have taken otherwise. For example, when a pastor looks out over his congregation on Sunday morning, he sees and reacts to people and their needs while he is preaching. Over in the corner sits a mother with a gloomy face and the corners of her mouth turned down. An alert pastor knows she's depressed, or at least discouraged, and his heart goes out to her. "What can I say that would lighten that load she carries?" he wonders to himself as he says a silent prayer. Then those noisy teenagers toward the back of the sanctuary break the preacher's train of thought. "Do I speak to their parents later and resist the temptation to call them down right now?" A man shaking his head back and forth arrests his attention. "I guess he's telling me he doesn't agree with the point I'm making right now. I'll try to talk to him later."

These and many other factors that happen during the preaching event can and do alter the direction and content of the sermon as it is being preached. A sensitive pastor will be alert to these factors and to the Spirit's leading during the preaching service. No TV program has ever been Spirit filled or guided in this sense.

Even without this interaction between people and preacher, the Spirit alone may edit the message. The preacher who has preached for any length of time knows that the message on paper he took into the pulpit and the message he proclaimed are rarely identical. Things got changed somewhere between page and proclamation. The Holy Spirit guides the Spirit-controlled preacher to add, delete, and change words and illustrations as the sermon is preached.

The reality of this Spirit-editing ministry is a sermon enhanced in value and usefulness and endowed as a living thing with a life and identity of its own. Nonexistent before the proclamation and part of history when finished, the sermon enjoys life only while being declared. For those who listen to a live taping of a message intended for rebroadcast, this revising work of the Spirit holds true because for them it is a live sermon, authentic and not artificial. This living dimension of the message, however, is untrue for the canned and rebroadcast version.

The televised message is a frozen proclamation. The Holy Spirit's editing work from page to proclamation is excluded. TV forbids it. It provides a record of what the Holy Spirit did in the past. But in no sense is it equivalent to the living empowerment of the Spirit during the actual process of the proclamation in the present. Each word, facial expression, and gesture remain forever unalterable. The televised message can still bless lives and save souls if God so wills, but it belongs in a different category of communication than its original.

The assembled believers are indwelt by the Holy Spirit.
   The third difference in the Holy Spirit's ministry relates to the congregation. We already have cited the Holy Spirit's ministry of unction upon the preacher and His presence as required for true worship. What is His influence upon the assembled body of believers? How does His ministry to the congregation differ in the televised sermon from His ministry during the same message when originally preached live?

   Usually alone, or at best with one or two others, the viewer of televised preaching remains isolated from the assembly. The informal atmosphere of people watching TV could hardly be characterized as "assembled" for much of anything other than entertainment. Viewing TV in this detached context bypasses the corporate indwelling and consequent blessing of the Spirit. Since the viewer has no connection with the whole congregation, he is an unaccompanied spectator, not a group participant.

   Mighty movings of the Spirit recorded in Acts 4:23–31 happened when the church assembled together for prayer and proclamation. These conditions and expectations prevail today.

> And when they had prayed, the place was shaken where they were assembled together; and they were all filled with the Holy Ghost, and they spake the word of God with boldness (v. 31).

   Since the Holy Spirit is omnipresent, His presence with the individual Christian watching TV cannot be denied, yet apart from the assembled church His ministry has been diminished. He may teach the individual even when alone, but other benefits of His unction upon corporate worship should not be expected.

Preaching Can Be Authentic, Not Artificial
   "We'll stay in touch so you stay in touch," say the news anchors from the coasts; but how can TV celebrities

thousands of miles away be more "in touch" than a pastor who lives and breathes among the very people to whom he preaches? Preaching ministers from a context of real personal contact, not pretend media relationships. Robert Schuller can't really care about each of his viewers or even know them, but real pastors can.

In contrast to the artificial world of TV, preaching really can be "in touch." Genuinely in touch implies two things which are impossible for TV—the ability to speak to your people with insight because you understand their struggles, both public and private, and the ability to prepare relevant sermons tailored to their narrowly focused needs. Pastors simply can't fix what they don't know is broken, but the knowledgeable preacher who is in touch with his flock can offer answers for hurting people.

One parody on "out of touch" teaching comes from a cartoon about a distraught husband and father talking to his pastor. "Pastor, my wife says she's leaving, my daughter is pregnant and on drugs, my business is going bankrupt. Pastor, I've just got to know which position is correct—pre-mill, post-mill, or a-mill?"

Because a pastor by definition is caring for the well-being of his people, an out-of-touch pastor is a contradiction of terms. Cold, aloof, impersonal, rigid, and ignorant of the needs of his congregation, the out-of-touch preacher mirrors TV's weaknesses without displaying its strengths. This preacher guarantees preaching that's a homiletical Titanic searching for an iceberg. It's obvious that Paul did not fit into the above categories, for Acts 20:31 tells us he preached night and day with tears as evidence of his involvement, knowledge, and concern for his flock. Apparently, being in touch gave his preaching authenticity.

Secondly, preaching can interact with its hearers on a two-way instead of a one-way street. For example, real preachers can show spontaneity, that is, the ability to interact with people during the preaching event.

Unexpected things happened to Jesus during preaching services—one day the roof caved in as a man came through the ceiling on a stretcher, other times angry Pharisees hurled angry objections at Him, demons exited their victims in His presence, and so on. None of these spontaneous interruptions troubled the Savior; on the contrary, showing marvelous flexibility, He used them as spontaneous teaching opportunities. No one accused Him of being out of touch. A pastor must carefully expunge all those out-of-touch elements from his sermons which kill his preaching's spontaneity.

Recently, while preaching on child discipline, a little four-year-old sitting in our congregation with his parents heard me describe the sound of a spanking as "boom, boom!" He immediately cried out loud, "Boom, boom, boom!" The church roared; then I said, "Now there's a young man who knows what I'm talking about!" The entire episode smacked with the quality of real life and the spontaneity characteristic of genuine interaction among the people of God.

Preaching Can Show Depth and Accuracy

"A picture is worth a thousand words." So goes one old saying that simply isn't true. Here is a fascinating, true story from November of 1991 which illustrates the accuracy of words over images.

TV viewers across the country were startled by a news bulletin in which ABC News anchor Peter Jennings announced that they were receiving reports of unusual air activity in the Persian Gulf. Some network affiliates in Boston, Pittsburgh, El Paso, Texas, and elsewhere had mistakenly re-run the original January 17 bulletin announcing the beginning of the air war. The tape was being sent to a New York station as a file tape. Some of the engineers at the affiliates were only *watching the video and not listening to the audio*. They saw the special report slide and put it on the air. After about ten seconds tjeu realized what had happened and bailed out.

What did they see? Images on a TV screen without words to explain them. This error came as a result of viewing pictures without the benefit of verbal interpretation. How long would people watch TV without sound? Turn the sound off for five minutes then ask, "How

> "Words may not be much to look at—and seem even less to hear—but compared to pictures they're as accurate as a laser beam."

much of the meaning have I lost?" Wordless TV leaves viewers wondering what's happening. To correctly evaluate pictures apart from words borders on the impossible. Nearly any interpretation can be placed on such images. Words without images, as in preaching, may seem boring, but images without words are imprecise and open to unlimited error. Preaching exhibits the strength of words without the inaccuracies of image-only communication. Words may not be much to look at—and seem even less to hear—but compared to pictures they're as accurate as a laser beam. Scripture devotes dozens of verses to the accuracy and power of spoken words. Not one reference commends the accuracy of images. Proverbs 18:21 tells us, "Death and life are in the power of the tongue (i.e. words): and they that love it shall eat the fruit thereof."

Consequently, pictures and sounds, as in TV and video, may elicit quick emotional responses on a surface level for the short term. But God designed preaching, as He did all verbal communication, to engage and penetrate the mind at a level of depth that TV can never match or even approach.God created human beings in His image and designed us to be deeply influenced by words. When God instituted language on the first day of Creation, Genesis 1:5 tells us, "And God called the light Day, and the darkness he called Night." Using words, God labelled His creation. God would not be God if He did not speak. Christ is called the Word of God, and as the Logos, He reveals Himself through words.

As the eternal Logos of God, the Lord Jesus Christ has ever been the expression, or manifestation, of God—the *living* Word of God, as the Bible is the *written* Word of God.1

By providing us with a Bible in the form of divinely inspired words, God has indicated His preference over all other forms of communication. How clearly God Himself has stated these principles in His Word.

> Heaven and earth shall pass away, but my words shall not pass away (Matt. 24:35).

> For verily I say unto you, Till heaven and earth pass, one jot or one tittle shall in no wise pass from the law, till all be fulfilled (Matt. 5:18).

Preaching enjoys unique superiority over TV. It has the ability to distinguish between different hearers, is empowered by the Spirit, is based upon real personal relationships, and is accurate. Why then does preaching often seem so limpid and forlorn while TV garners such excitement? Part of the answer must be that we have not fully appreciated nor employed preaching's strong, distinctive traits. David's sling, if left dangling at his side, would never bring the giant down. We will now focus on how to use the distinctive powers of preaching to their greatest advantage and precisely where TV is weak.

Personalize Your Applications by Targeting and Shaping

To reach the audiences that advertisers want, broadcasters use the strategy of *targeting*, choosing programs that appeal to those subsets of the mass audience that are most likely to buy the advertisers' products. The need to reach large numbers of the people willing and able to pay the bills, whether as advertisers or subscribers, has led to targeting and segmentation throughout the electronic media.[2]

Effective preaching to TV-saturated mentalities becomes personal to your audience by directly addressing different kinds of hearers and shaping content to meet their individual needs. This distinctive strength elevates preaching above TV in power, impact, and appeal. So the principle here is simple but profound: on Sunday morning either you target your people group and shape the application or they'll tune you out.

Personalize your applications by targeting and shaping them for specific people groups. Observe how the apostle Paul personalized his applications in 1 Thessalonians 5:14 (NASV):

> And we urge you, brethren, **admonish** the *unruly*, **encourage** the *fainthearted*, **help** the *weak*, **be patient** with *all men* (1 Thes. 5:14 nasv).

Here Paul cites four distinct categories, or targets, and shapes a message particular to each. He targets the "unruly" for admonition. Clearly, however, we don't admonish the next category, but rather we "encourage" the fainted hearted.

Mixing up these groups is counterproductive, since the "weak" need support not confrontation. Likewise, targeting and shaping recognize certain truths apply equally to all people. For example, in the fourth category, Paul says "be patient" with all men. No need to target a special application here!

Failure to follow these Biblical principles creates loathsome generic applications and accounts for lost ministry, disillusioned people, and ineffective preaching. Application without destination is doomed to oblivion.

TV has practiced this targeting principle for so long and our congregations are so accustomed to it that they expect targeted communication and respond accordingly. We must never forget that this very issue of targeting is one of the major concerns of broadcasters in general and commercial programmers in particular.

To target the audience, preachers need to follow this two-step process:

1. To what group of persons does this truth apply?
2. What must they do after they hear it?

Answering these two simple questions about who you're speaking to and what they're to do will make your applications useful to the congregation far beyond the ordinary generic types that mirror TV. Until the preacher can satisfactorily answer these two basic questions, he isn't ready to prepare the applications for his sermon.

In Ephesians, for example, identical doctrine merits

Targeting	Shaping Application
Husbands,	love
Wives,	submit
Children,	obey
Parents,	don't provoke your children, instead bring them up
Servants,	be obedient to your masters
Masters,	refrain from threatening but treat your servants instead with justice

personalized applications shaped for different groups with varied needs. After three chapters of doctrine with no distinctions, Paul targets individual categories and shapes differing applications for each category when applying the doctrine in chapter 5.

Preaching can and should discriminate among its hearers into applicational groupings: the young, the retired, the single, the married, the worried, the depressed, the fearful, the immoral. Although TV marketing strategies attempt to focus on specific target groups, none of these categories is discernible from behind a TV screen; but from behind the pulpit they are.

Jay Adams suggests that the wise pastor analyze his audience using formal and informal contacts, counseling, input from his leadership, plus any other legitimate means of determining applicational groups within his church.[3] Haddon Robinson, as part of his sermon preparation, surrounds himself with an invisible congregation composed of the different people groups within his church in order to analyze their responses to his sermon and determine his preaching strategy.[4] Tim Keller insists on audience analysis that adapts to the listeners' frames of reference; he has provided outstanding examples of these different frames of reference in the form of a chart including dozens of "possible people groups" in an audience.[5]

In targeting the people groups during the sermon, I often use these phrases, or words to this effect:

- Many of you . . .
- yet others . . .
- but some . . .

For example, "Many fathers here this morning are doing a great job. You're hitting consistent singles. Others of you strike out from time to time, but get back into the game as soon as possible. Some fathers here, however, don't even get up to bat. You've dropped out of the game altogether, and don't even bother to leave the dugout. If you're one of these, I have good news for you—there's hope for beleaguered dads." Just accurately defining their problem gives them hope—"That's me, that's what I am, a beleaguered dad." Don't fear to lose the rest of your hearers outside your target group. You won't. They want to know what you have to say to others as well as what you'll say to them.

Narrowing your focus of application automatically engages entire categories of persons otherwise missed. When they hear you call their number—financially troubled? ... discouraged wife, ... confused teenager, ... discouraged person, ... depressed person, ... you who are gripped by fear, ... greedy, ... gripped by a habit, ... trouble with the boss at work?—they tune in for the message. These are only a few of the ways to target and shape your message. Each preacher can invent creative ways of targeting that will multiply his effectiveness to people who are as different as their fingerprints.

This isn't preaching at individuals, rather it's preaching that prints an address on the letter so the postman knows where to deliver it, and more importantly, the occupants know that it's been delivered. If someone criticizes, "You were preaching at me," my reply is, "Only wear the shoe if it fits; if it doesn't fit, don't wear it."

Every listener seeks and sorts while both TV and the preacher attempt to connect. When TV doesn't discriminate (target and shape) for them, viewers will do it for themselves. This is the driving force behind the practice of "grazing." Studies show, for example, that women watch certain programs men won't. Single women watch different TV from married women, and why wouldn't they? They're different people with varying interests, needs, and concerns. This difference is also true for men, boys, and the elderly. Preaching needs to connect with each group at some point; different groups in your congregation need to know you have something specific to say to them.

> **"The data you gain from this listener profile will guide you in targeting and shaping truth to various people groups having a variety of needs. This gives you a definite edge over TV."**

Listener Profiles Help to Target and Shape

As the failure of a fighter pilot to accurately target his object accounts for significant "collateral damage," so failure in preaching to properly target people groups can produce similar effects. For example, you're trying to reach that selfish guy who hoards his money and never gives. So in preaching you exhort the church about the importance of giving. Afterward, your most unselfish, sensitive couple approaches with that wilted look. "We already give more than a tithe, should we be giving more?" You know they shouldn't, you weren't even aiming for them, yet they're victims of friendly fire.

How much do you know about the people to whom you preach? Since knowing your listener and having an impact on your listener increase in direct proportion to each other, knowing your listeners is key to successful application.

Persons in each of the following categories have distinctive prejudices, viewpoints, and concerns. These significant distinctions should alter applications of truth to life. The data you gain from this listener profile will guide you in targeting and shaping truth to various people groups having a variety of needs. *This gives you a definite edge over TV.* Here are one dozen of the most crucial areas.

1. *Name and address*—both of these have impact on how people see themselves and what their views on money and church expenditures will be.
2. *Married or single*—divorced or remarried, other than saved or unsaved, this is probably the most determinative data in analyzing needs.
3. *Occupation*—blue collar, white collar, years on job, tenure, accountant, engineer, nurse, teacher, businessman, etc.
4. *Achievements*—professional, personal, recognition within community.
5. *Children*—how many and what ages, spiritual condition.
6. *Educational level*—high school, college, graduate degrees; special training such as the marines, CIA, IRS, FBI gives clues on how they view government and authority.

7. *Previous church background*—alerts you in handling key words and doctrines that might be misunderstood, for example Roman Catholic terminology.
8. *Health and medical history*—poor health creates a different set of needs from healthy listeners.
9. *Hobbies*—leisure time activities are outstanding sources of illustrations, examples, and stories that people will listen to when they will hear nothing else.
10. *Political associations*—key issues, ignorance or inattention to these often gets a preacher in or out of "hot water."
11. *Personal goals for career and family*—progress toward goals is a big matter; their position and direction on the corporate ladder makes a difference in how some listeners hear and respond to preaching.
12. *Spiritual gifts*—Christians with the gift of mercy, for example, often have some different needs from the prophet and the exhorter.

I have new members fill out a data sheet that provides information in many of these categories. When I stumble finding applications, I pull these sheets and think about to whom I'm ministering. The more I know about them, the more effectively I can target whatever truth I'm preaching and shape its application to fit their needs.

When deciding what shows to sponsor and which programing will draw the people group they have targeted, ad agencies take these factors seriously in their marketing strategies. Pastors must also. Vigorous preaching that connects with people will build up the church, but failure here on the preacher's part accounts for loss of robust preaching and lumps us together with impersonal, inaccurate, unreal TV. Targetless preaching offers nothing different to TV-conditioned mentalities than what already bores them, since TV so often tries to entertain us but fails miserably. Authentic Spirit-empowered preaching rises above limp and pointless TV, penetrates TV-saturated mentalities, and elevates preaching to its maximum effectiveness.

In addition, powerful, personalized applications go a long way to keep boredom down, our goal for the next chapter.

CHAPTER EIGHT

Purge Boredom Factors

If the Surgeon General had to report the leading cause of death in church, it would no doubt result in a new warning label being placed on some sermons: "Warning: this sermon may be hazardous to your spiritual health."

Listening to some preachers should be outlawed as cruel and unusual punishment. Their preaching resembles winter. The congregation's eyes freeze over like the lakes, their heads go down as the birds fly south, and just like bears that hibernate, their minds enter a state of suspended animation for the duration of the message. Frozen preachers produce frozen people.

According to Webster's dictionary, *to bore* means "to auger through or to make a hole by hollowing out an empty place, hence a place where there is nothing." Boredom is a condition where nothing exists but emptiness—no life, no excitement, no change, no nothing. Boredom often describes preaching.

What are the boredom factors according to programmed people? How does the faithful pastor eliminate boredom? Why does one preacher capture and hold the attention of his listeners while another doesn't? Is it natural gifts, background, training, or other unidentified factors? Or does one preacher observe certain principles of communication while another preacher does not?

Yes, there are key principles of communication that can keep your congregation wide awake. These principles are designed for preaching to the TV mentalities described earlier in chapter 4:

- the visually oriented listener with the problem of evoked recall
- the passive nonresponder
- the attention-deficit adult plagued by grazing, passive alpha sequencing, and decontextualization.

Take heart—there are effective solutions to these debilitating factors, and boring preaching can become interesting and exciting, even for programmed people.

Avoid the Three Unpardonable Sins

There are three surefire errors in preaching guaranteed to bore programmed people to tears: immobility in delivery, imageless words for illustrations, and abstract content unrelated to real life. If you want to swap boredom for excitement and generate attention, interest, and enthusiasm in your listeners, you must replace those staples with new approaches.

To say it from the positive standpoint:

- Be mobile when you preach.
- Be picturesque when you illustrate.
- Be real when you chose your subject matter.

Violate these principles at your peril or employ them for your success. Let's see why they work and then learn how to apply them.

Be Mobile in Your Delivery

The average scene change during primetime TV is once every 3.7 seconds. Why do producers change the camera angle, the person who is talking, the setting, or the scenery so frequently? Because it keeps their viewers glued to the screen. Anticipating the next event, fear of missing an important fact, wondering what will happen next all combine to bolster attention and interest. *Moving objects generate attention.*

An immobile image will not hold the attention of persons who are accustomed to motion. All week our hearers are used to staring at moving images. As shown in chapter 4, people's eyeballs move little while watching TV; they stare at the set as a fixed object while the images do the moving.

Test this fact for yourself. With the TV on and friends or family members watching a favorite program, position yourself beside them in such a way that you can see both their eyes and the TV screen. Notice that the back and forth movements of their eyes do not track parallel with the movements of the images on the screen. To do so would be impossible because the speed and sequencing of the images is far too rapid. There is not a one-to-one ratio between eye motion and image motion. Only slight eye movements occur in people watching TV from fixed positions because the TV set is a nonmoving object.

Try staring at a fixed point for ten seconds without moving your eyes. Tiring, isn't it? Now look toward the same point again, but instead of staring, move your eyes from object to object for the same ten seconds. Notice the difference? It's far easier to move your eyes than to stare. TV magnifies this effect. Images move automatically for the TV viewer. In church, when staring at a pastor, nothing moves if he doesn't. While the congregation continues to stare, you must provide the movement. In the same way that TV's sequence of images maintains their attention, your meaningful movement while preaching will have the same effect by:

- suggesting a sequence,
- anticipating the next event,
- keeping them watching for fear of missing anything.

Never forget that while preaching, you are being watched as well as listened to. If Paul in Acts 21:40 "beckoned with his hands" to increase his effectiveness, so can you.

Dramatic increase in the attention of all your listeners can be achieved through meaningful movement. In fact, to capture and hold the attention of the visually oriented listener, meaningful movement is a must.

Maintain the attention of the visually oriented listener by:

1. Walking

a) Walking from side to side on the platform demonstrates contrast. Keep in mind that logical and temporal movement for an audience or congregation is from left to right. When you say, "Don't do this!" walk to the left side of platform. When you say, "Instead, do this!" walk to the right side. Your actions illustrate the truth while the audience watches. They're listening and learning at the same time.

b) Backing away from the pulpit shows impact or alienation. As the preacher steps further and further away and puts distance between himself and audience, he shows how sin separates us from God and others, etc.

c) Moving closer to the audience is more personal. People wake up when a preacher leaves his spot from behind the pulpit and comes around front lifting his hands and saying, "People, listen to me!" His actions and his words send the same message, "I'm reaching out to you." Naturally, they'll reach back. Behind the pulpit is the place for teaching; moving toward them is more personal and better suited for applying.

2. Gesturing

- Expressive use of the arms, face, and hands invigorates truth with action, commands attention, and magnetizes your hearers.
- One hand held out to your side with fingers pointing indicates direction—"go ye."
- Both hands held up, palms open, indicates alarm, shock, surprise.
- The head hung down, chin to chest, shows shame, discouragement, or despair.
- A clenched fist shows vengeance, judgment, anger.
- Open palms pointing down indicate surrender or friendship, etc.

3. Striking a Pose

- Arms crossed covering your face demonstrate hiding, fear, and danger.

- Arms in a criss-crossing motion mean negative, no, or rejection.
- Arms bent at the elbow and crossed over the chest with your hands on your shoulders show selfishness—focus on me, me, me.
- Strolling or waving are also movements that attract attention.

Try an experiment. Different parts of the country, different ethnic groups, various cultures, and rural or urban areas all have different twists that must be learned. Have a trusted leader or friend evaluate your movements while you preach. Set up categories for effectiveness such as:

- How does my movement from behind the pulpit to along side it come across you?
- When I move closer to the people, what impression does it convey?
- When I make this motion, *(example)*, does it reinforce my point?

Let the content determine the degree of movement. Don't go overboard. A constant flow of meaningless gestures that are unrelated to the content will detract, not add, to your effectiveness. Finding the balance may seem elusive, but it's a highly worthy goal. Pursue it!

Use Word Pictures in Your Delivery

Using the right word calls forth images in the mind's eye of the hearer and can make a powerful impact. If you want your hearers to see what you see, then you must "fax it" to them using words; these are the only tools the preachers has. Likewise, the only pictures they'll see are the ones you draw for them using specific, concrete, and detailed words. By *word pictures* I mean verbal descriptions of physical images.

Scripture often draws word pictures, especially of abstract truths like righteousness, guilt, and forgiveness. In the following two verses from Isaiah, see how righteousness is a garment; forgiveness, a washing.

But we are all as an unclean thing [diseased person], and all our righteousnesses are as filthy rags; and we all do fade as a leaf; and our iniquities, like the wind, have taken us away (Isaiah 64:6).

[T]hough your sins be as scarlet, they shall be as white as snow; though they be red like crimson, they shall be as wool (Isaiah 1:18)

Jesus used parables about people, flowers, and children playing in the marketplace. He described in detail a funeral procession and a tower falling on unsuspecting victims and drew brief word pictures like "as a hen gathers her chicks." Such scenes indelibly etched His messages into the minds of those who heard Him.

Picturing truth so that it is visible turns the mind into a picture gallery instead of a dictionary. Preachers who tap this resource strengthen the impact of their sermons whether the word pictures come as phrases, a couple of sentences, or extended descriptions.

Phrases and Sentences

Painting word pictures is easy and fun. For example, if I wanted to turn "he was strong and dangerous" into a word picture, I might say, "The man is a human bulldozer; he flattens everybody who gets in his way." If I am painting a word picture of a critical woman, I might say, "Her tongue is a chainsaw." The physical image translates the intangible qualities into something concrete your hearers can see in their minds. You can determine which physical images bring abstractions into concrete realities by using these three steps:

1. Determine the quality or truth you wish to communicate. For example,
   a) Trouble is reliable
   b) Christ's willingness to die

2. Reduce it to one concept such as
   a) Reliability
   b) Meekness

3. Survey the dictionary, the thesaurus, or other sources and choose one physical image that most powerfully

conveys the concept and "paint the picture":
a) Reliable—as a billcollector
b) Meek—as a puppy

As an experiment, I once examined a book of the Bible at random to see if it contained any word pictures. I chose Hosea because I was unfamiliar with it and thought there were no picturesque words or phrases in it. Here is what I found.

Hosea		
Chapter/Verse	**Quality/Concept**	**Word Picture**
1:10	Children as	Sand of the sea
2:3	Gomer is a	Wilderness, like a desert
2:6	Hedge her up with	Thorns
4:16	Israel is like a	Stubborn lamb
5:12, 14	The Lord is like a	Moth, rottenness, Lion
6:4	Your loyalty is like the	Morning clouds, dew
7:4, 6	The hearts of the wicked	like an Oven
7:8	Ephraim like a	Cake not turned
7:11–12	Ephraim like a Bring them down like the	Silly dove Birds
8:10	They have	Sown the wind
		Reaped the whirlwind
9:11	Ephraim's glory will	Fly away like a bird
10:11	Ephraim is	A trained heifer that loves to thresh

Extended Descriptions

Preachers can and must take lessons from award-winning books and songs such as Michael Shaara's Pulitzer Prize-winning novel about the Civil War, *The Killer Angels.* Just *listen* and you will *see* his descriptions of the army officers at the battle of Gettysburg.

> *Robert Edward Lee*, He is in his fifty-seventh year. Five feet ten inches tall but very short in the legs, so that when he rides a horse he seems much taller. Red-faced, like all the Lees, white-bearded, dressed in an old gray coat and a gray felt hat, without insignia, so that he is mistaken sometimes for an elderly major of dignity . . .
>
> *James Longstreet*, Lieutenant General, forty-two. Lee's second-in-command. A large man, larger than Lee, full-bearded, blue-eyed, ominous, slow-talking, crude. He is one of the first of the new soldiers, the cold-eyed men who have sensed the birth of the new war of machines.
>
> *George Pickett*, Major General, thirty-eight. Gaudy and lovable, long-haired, perfumed.
>
> *Richard Ewell*, Lieutenant General, forty-six. Egg-bald, one-legged, recently married.
>
> *Jubal Early*, Major General, forty-six. Commander of one of Ewell's divisions. A dark, cold, icy man, bitter, alone.
>
> *Winfield Scott Hancock*, Major General, thirty-nine. Armistead's old friend. A magnetic man with a beautiful wife. A painter of talent, a picture-book General. Has a tendency to gain weight, but at this moment he is still young and slim, still a superb presence, a man who arrives on the battlefield in spotlessly clean linen and never keeps his head down . . .[1]

Conjuring up such vivid images delights and captivates your audience and increases your effectiveness in preaching.

Be Real in Subject Matter

The TV-conditioned mentality exhibits a bias for experience over truth, so unless you have good reason to do otherwise, begin with real-life experiences, not doctrine. Why? Because TV is 90 percent experiences about people. To the TV mentality personal experience is more valid than truth. Therefore, it takes priority. Truth is not truth unless my experience validates it. Even Christian TV reflects this unbiblical perspective, as Quentin Schultze writes in a chapter entitled "TV and Evangelism: Unequally Yoked?"

Television's fundamental religious bias, then, is toward experientially validated theologies—those theologies whose veracity is communicated through the experiences of believers, not through doctrinal or even biblical certainty. For this reason, many televangelists use their lives to interpret the Bible, not their Bible to interpret their lives.[2]

Since this experience-based truth holds true for even Christian mentalities, imagine how accurately it characterizes nonchurched folks. Since abandoning propositional truth, our culture is experiencing the aftermath of an empirical philosophy that subordinates truth to personal experience. This subordination results in the priority of experience over truth. Beginning a sermon with experience is starting at a point of strength and interest. It enables the preacher to lead his hearers to truth.

Often we must begin on the feeling and experience level in order to involve an entire generation of persons for whom experience is the acid test. Many listeners, when unable to relate your preaching to their personal experience, refuse to listen for long. The principle is: begin with experience then move to truth. But the beginning matters as much as the direction.

Preaching that's real begins at the intersection of truth and life, where the circle of truth overlaps with life's experiences. Preach to people about themselves, evaluated and interpreted by the Bible. Your listeners should be able, during a sermon, to look at the verse and at the same time point to an area, or areas, in their lives that the verse touches. Preaching that is real is a wedding of the Bible and life where the bride and the groom, truth and experience, embrace in plain sight. Obtaining results in preaching to the TV mindset takes both experience and truth—both, not either or.

So much preaching is like a boy who sits on the handlebars of his buddy's bicycle, goes around the block for a ride, and then is dropped off at the exact spot where he started. Real preaching, however, changes, moves, enlightens, and heals but never leaves people where it found them. It conforms its hearers to the character of Christ.

The following chart offers a system for determining topics for both expository and topical messages. It begins with both the experiences of life and areas relevant to the spiritual progress of the church (not the interests of the pastor or the latest hot theological issue). Experience-related content interpreted within a biblical framework draws upon the strengths of both. In other words, real preaching begins where people are but doesn't leave them at that point. It transfers them to the higher ground where God wants them to be.

Follow the A-B-C Method		
A. Identify where the congregation is in their spiritual maturity for a specific area, i.e. evangelism, prayer, Bible study	**B.** Preaching content should **move them from A to C**, i.e. from where they are to where God wants them to be. What will is take **content-wise** to make this transition?	**C.** Define where God wants them to be in this area. Be specific.
1. Prayer—Many in our church have consistent prayer lives, and yet less that half the congregation attends our prayer service. This needs work!	1. _____ _____ _____ _____ _____	1. Prayer—Words that describe godly prayer: believing, faithful, unselfish, etc.
2. Evangelism—How can we ever think we have arrived when there are so many lost and needy people all around us. It has been too long since the waters of baptism have been stirred. We need a series on personal witnessing if we are to be the church God talked about in Matt. 28:19–20.	2. _____ _____ _____ _____ _____	2. Evangelism—God wants every growing member of the body of Christ to share the Good News effectively.
3. Bible study—Several women enjoy Bible studies, but our men seem backward about this . . .	3. _____ _____ _____ _____	3. Bible Study—2 Tim. 2:15 says that all believers must study to show themselves approved of God and handle properly the Word of Truth.

CHAPTER NINE

Preaching to Programmed People

I have suggested that preaching should respond to the challenge of TV in three main ways:

1. by capitalizing on TV's power to place images and words into the minds of our congregations
2. by employing preaching's distinctive strengths in contrast to TV's weaknesses
3. by ridding preaching of common practices that turn off and turn away programmed people

Those who would reach the various listeners of our day must

- penetrate their minds
- stimulate their affections
- persuade their wills

To accomplish this, you must get your listeners to do at least three things:

- think your thoughts with you
- accept what they hear
- reach similar conclusions.

The preacher lays the track; the audience follows along in the train in hopes of arriving at the destination where understanding awaits them. During this journey, however, some trains of thought derail, others will take sidetracks, while a small percentage will wreck completely. The preacher's goal is to get as many on board as possible and deliver every passenger safely. By recognizing and following certain guidelines for structuring the sermon, effective preaching to programmed people will limit losses and increase the impact of the message.

Here are five principles designed to meet the needs of TV-conditioned listeners.

Principle One: Make Points with Brevity

Shorten up those extended explanations. State your point within one hundred seconds. If this seems impossible, remember your congregation has logged thousands of hours watching and listening to TV commercials. The majority are no longer than twenty-seven seconds. If the commercial world can gain attention, spark the inter-

> "Brevity is the kinsman of clarity and the mother of all impact; don't drag out your points."

est, give direction, and call for a response from your congregation within such limits, why can't preachers employ a similar economy of words? Listen to good radio preachers for examples. On-the-air time is money, so they make words count. Respect words enough to spend them wisely.

The volume and velocity of information on TV produces a mindset with amazing powers of discrimination. Rambling, redundant, wordy preachers bore programmed people for the same reason they're bored with TV. They detest being buried under a mountain of meaningless information.

On an average people can listen to 350–400 words-per-minute, while preachers speak only 150 words-per-minute. Our hearers wander around in this 200 words gap and get lost. Brevity is the kinsman of clarity and the mother of all impact; *don't drag out your points.*

Following this principle of brevity does not result in watered-down preaching that's doctrinally anemic or in simple, short sermons. It doesn't reinforce the audience's difficulty in concentrating. It simply requires making the same points more concisely, like eating the same meal with smaller bites. How do you eat an elephant? One bite at a time. The point is come to the point! Say it! Or as Max Lucado has said,

> Here's a toast to the simple sentence. Here's a salute to one-liners. Join me in applauding the delete key and the eraser. I believe in brevity. Cut the fat and keep the fact. Give us words to chew on, not words to wade through. . . . Bareknuckle it. Concise (but not shallow). Vivid (but not detailed).[1]

Observing this principle means ruthlessly purging filler phrases such as "Time won't permit me to" and apologetic discourses during the introduction focused on the preacher, his health, his voice, his need. What purpose is served by saying, "I've had alot of interruptions in my study this week but one thing I have learned is . . . ." Don't tell us about your week unless it makes a contribution to your point. If you have a cold, so what? Those who detect it will understand, and for the ones who don't, why bother? Extraneous data only weaken and clutter up the message; rabbit trails lose people. Although Jesus had infinite wisdom and could have delivered complex sermons, His messages were characteristically clear and simple—the common people heard Him gladly.

Some preachers delight in repeating the same truth the same way in the identical words for no reason. Such repetition wastes words and communicates to hearers that the message has little value. Be brief.

Rid your preaching vocabulary of inept structures and

wasted words for the same reason you clean out the garage or empty the trash. Such poor stewardship of time and energy serves no purpose. In fact, it's harmful since it blunts the force of the message. Go through your bag of homiletical phrases and identify all the worthless jargon and meaningless filler phases. Clean house!

The standard homiletical approaches are effective if done with brevity. The *state, illustrate, explain,* and *apply* approach works fine and, if employed with brevity, keeps listeners tracking with the preacher. If you can state your point within two minutes, take an additional two or less to illustrate it, then explain and apply it in under eight minutes, your impact will dramatically increase over the drawn-out approach requiring three or four minutes to accomplish each part. In a properly structured sermon each point will take between five and eight minutes to state, illustrate, explain, and apply. Of course this form can vary according to the sermon's purpose and the individual tastes of the preacher, but it still should equal three times eight or twenty-four minutes. The introduction uses three minutes and so does the conclusion, adding up to a total sermon of thirty minutes. Violate these limits and the message sags, lacks development, fails to flow, and goes nowhere. Programmed people detect this lack of progress and tune out, saying to themselves, "Nothing's happening here. Why stay tuned?"

Variations on this theme, like stretching out the application for a how-to sermon or enlarging the teaching content for a doctrinal message, can change this size. The minimum is thirty minutes, however, and the maximum is forty-five. If you preach less than thirty minutes, you've got time you're not using; if more than forty-five, you using time you haven't got. People will stay, but their thoughts will stray.

Principle Two: Keep Listeners Tracking with You

Pastors are horrified to learn that what someone understood them to say was the opposite of what they actually said. Where do these communication anomalies come from? Sometimes they are simply the result of the problems of verbal communication that have always been present. Sometimes they are the direct result of poor communication by the pastor. Sometimes they are the direct result of TV saturation. Because the grazing minds of attention-deficit adults fade in and out of the sermon, they absorb distortions, fragmented understandings, and outright misunderstandings.

Pastors must face it. Preacher's words and the ears and minds of their hearers don't track side by side. Hearing patterns are skewed, zigzagged, or even off on tangents. They ricochet like bullets. They tune in and out, daydreaming, stopping, then starting in fits and sputters. This is one of the effects of media upon preaching—conditional listening. When you fail to meet their conditions, they tune you out, graze, drop through the cracks, and get lost. To avoid this problem preachers must:

- answer objections as soon as possible
- limit switchbacking
- build sturdy transitions

Answer objections as soon as possible.

To anticipate objections and provide timely responses during the course of the sermon enhances preaching power. Try to answer objections early in the message. It's pointless to continue when the audience's understanding is knotted and tangled. Why? Because they won't wait twenty minutes for the answer. If an objection is not answered within a maximum of two minutes, you've probably lost them. When the mind of your hearers ceases to track with the logic of the message, the force of the message goes on hold. Like a rubberband, their patience will stretch only so far before it snaps and you lose them.

In 1 Corinthians 15:35–36 Paul followed this principle immediately after making his point about the reality of the resurrection:

> But some man will say, How are the dead raised up? and with what body do they come? Thou fool, that which thou sowest is not quickened, except it die.

Limit switchbacking.

How often in the course of a sermon must the audience look down at the printed page to follow along in their own Bibles, look up toward the visual image of the preacher, then back and forth again? This is called switchbacking, and this transition from print to moving image raises a roadblock to peripheral listeners. They often lose momentum in the switch between differing forms—from image to print and from print to image. Since its overall effect weakens the sermon, switchbacking should be limited.

To avoid the loss of scriptural authority, preachers ought to read the sermon text near the beginning of the message—usually after having begun with some real-life experience. During the course of the sermon, however, it is more effective to quote the Scripture for hearers than to direct them to read it for themselves. Why? Many earnest Christians simply can't switch from looking at and listening to the preacher to finding the appropriate chapter and verse in their Bibles without losing their train of thought. Once their minds have "uncoupled" the cars on the train, so to speak, it is difficult to "recouple" them.

If listeners must have a direct quote from the Scripture, read or quote it for them instead of requiring them to read it for themselves. Doing this retains more hearers and enables them to *keep tracking with you.*

Build sturdy transitions.

Coupling sermon points together by using transitional statements strengthens attentiveness, intensifies the force of the logic, and heightens the authority of the argument. Decontextualized thinkers rarely feel the sweep and flow of a sermon's momentum without the aid of transitions because they don't think contextually and therefore can't associate related truths. They drop out, so to speak.

> "Without transitions many listeners hear only three or four short sermons that happen to be put back to back instead of one long message organically connected."

Transitions prevent dropouts. They compel truths to be related by showing the relationship existing between them. Without transitions many listeners hear only three or four short sermons that happen to be put back to back instead of one long message organically connected.

For example, in Romans chapters 3–5 the apostle Paul builds the case for the lostness of mankind because of the absence of any possible righteousness before God. In 3:10 he says, "As it is written, There is none righteous, no, not one." With no hope of human works providing a righteousness acceptable to God, the only possible solution is a righteousness that comes by faith. So the preaching points might look like this:

I. The righteousness of man is unable to save him, since all are under sin and therefore unrighteous (Rom. 3:9–20)
II. Only a God-kind of righteousness (i.e. a righteousness acceptable to God) can save (Rom. 3:21–26).
III. This kind of righteousness comes only by faith in Jesus Christ, not by works (Rom.4:1–5:1).

The transition between points I and II might look like this:

Because man is unable to save himself (a restatement of point one in a slightly different form), he stands in need of a larger and greater righteousness that can. That's why we need God's righteousness; our own is insufficient (an explanation linking the points), so we're forced to find an adequate righteousness—one that God will accept. In other words, our failure forces us to seek a source beyond ourselves (restatement in different terms). "Now, only a God-kind of righteousness can save" (this final transition sentence leads the hearers into the second point).

Such a transition links the points by showing *why*. It is a *causal* transition.

The transition between points II and III might look like this:

Man's deep need for a divinely given righteousness (summary of point II) can be fulfilled in only one way, by faith in Jesus Christ (paraphrase of point III). For only in Him can we have a righteousness that's acceptable to God. Any other righteousness, any other faith, or any other way (relates all three points together in a summary fashion showing their interrelation and similarities) is unacceptable to God.

Transitions may tell why, what, or how, but they always define and link the main points together in solid fashion. Using these "thought bridges," the preacher can keep listeners tracking with him during the sermon.

Principle Three: Round Up Strays

Because of grazing, decontextualization, and attention-deficit adults, the need frequently arises to regather the lost and straying despite the best efforts of the most gifted preacher. Eyes and ears were given to preachers as means of grace. When you see shuffling, uneasiness, and squirming and hear papers rattling, people whispering, and that rumbling kind of low buzzing-type noise, don't ignore it! Your listeners are telegraphing an important message. They're not with you! They're either confused about the meaning of the sermon or have given up. It's time to round up the strays.

Here are four ways to bring the herd together:

1. Carefully plan normal homiletical devices.
2. Restate the same content using different words.
3. Ask rhetorical questions.
4. Use sounds.

Carefully plan normal homiletical devices.

Illustrations, quotes, and legitimate stories about people, pets, and children can help round up strays, but all have one significant limitation—when given on the spur of the moment, they often don't fit and can easily become counterproductive. What's needed in this case are *predetermined* ways to regain lost listeners that don't have to be *preplaned* in such as way that they have to be used at one time only in the sermon. In other words, preachers need spontaneous illustrations that are usable like a spare tire, only when needed. When a preacher needs a roundup, he needs it badly, and it must be available to him, ready to use.

Restate the same content using different words.

At times during the sermon the preacher needs to restate the same content in a different way. For example,

Preaching point (James 1:2–4)—believers should be joyful in trials, knowing that trouble, if handled properly, makes us perfect and entire, lacking nothing.

Restatement of preaching point (in paraphrase)—In other words, you must see difficulty as the tool God uses to shape us into the image of Christ. Because of this need to be shaped into the image of Christ, you can decide to be upbeat even when it's tough.

Don't use identical words in a restatement. They didn't work the first time. Allow time to practice this skill outside the pulpit by using a thesaurus or better yet by teaching children's church where repeating the same truths in different ways comes automatically. Find a more picturesque, a more concrete, and a more memorable phrase; then say it again. Use Bible paraphrases. They're your best friends when looking for content repetition. A restatement from a paraphrase is far better than just telling a story that doesn't fit the context of the sermon just to win your listeners' attention. While the Bible is one internally consistent book, its truths are stated and restated in many different ways. Restating truths several different ways works in preaching also.

Ask rhetorical questions.

Never underestimate the cogency of well-phrased questions. Jesus said, "Whom do men say that I the Son of man am? . . . But whom say ye that I am?" (Matt. 16:13, 15) Ask a flurry of cluster questions. These questions, when delivered with inflection consistent with questions, act like metal to a magnet upon the minds of your listeners.

- "Isn't this true?"
- "What do you think?"
- "Does this make sense to you?"
- "Are you listening?"
- "Do you see?"
- "Should this matter?"

Question clusters gather those straying thoughts back into the fold.

Use sounds.

Consider the volume and variety of sounds from just a single TV program to see what our people are used to hearing and what preachers compete against.

In Acts 2:1–3 God displayed heaven's audiovisuals to gain Jerusalem's attention. Using the sound of a tornado (a rushing mighty wind) and visual images like "tongues" of fire worked then, and it still works today.

Think about the sound of the palms of your hands rubbing back and forth together beside the microphone, "whoosh, whoosh," or the "ssmat, smmaatt" sound as your fist strikes your open palm. The sound of your heels stomping on the platform, "thud, thud," can echo throughout the entire auditorium.

Does the use of sounds seem too risky? It might be interpreted by some as undignified, yet how dignified are sleeping parishioners? When employed appropriately, sounds enhance preaching. In *Preaching with Purpose*, Jay Adams says:

> There is a great, untapped resource here. The Greek sound *ouai*, translated "woe" in the New Testament (cf. Matt. 23), is more of an exclamation or groan of pain, displeasure, or anger than an actual word. This sound is interjected much the same way we use sounds like "ouch!" or "ahhh!" or "oh!" Jesus didn't hesitate to utter such sounds that have turned respectable by becoming words. Stiff professionals rarely even use them, let alone mere groans and other sound![2]

Principle Four: Give Your Audience Spontaneous Feedback

Why do talk show hosts speak to band members offstage or take their discussions into the audience? To involve the audience and thereby to gain their attention and interest.

One of preaching's distinctive strengths over TV is its flexibility. Use it—interact with the people. Preaching that employs feedback arouses, even electrifies, an audience. Talk to them about themselves.

- "Some of you look puzzled, worried, perplexed."
- "Does what I'm saying trouble you?"

- "Should this be important to you?"
- "Did I say something wrong? Did I say something right?"

Used with discernment, dialoguing with the audience arouses everyone's interest. In many churches preachers can still call for an "amen" from the congregation and get it. Whether or not that works in your church, the principle still stands—whenever possible, elicit from your audience the response that you seek.

If that won't work, another method will. Take a survey of your church on a topic of your choice. Use the results in the introduction of your message. "For example, 20 percent of you said it is possible to find peace during a divorce, 67 percent said it isn't possible, and 17 percent said they didn't know. Let's see what God said about peace in the midst of trouble."

Don't hibernate or give the audience the impression you're unaware of their responses. Give them feedback!

Principle Five: Challenge Them with the Consequences

Why do people change so little and so slowly? One reason we have shown is that TV has severed the information-response umbilical cord. So, reaching the passive nonresponder proves one of the toughest challenges confronting preachers today. Once again, the Master is the Master Preacher. Listen to Jesus in His Sermon on the Mount as He sweeps away every remnant of passivity in His hearers by spelling out the consequences of their actions:

> Therefore every one who hears these words of Mine and acts upon them, may be compared to a wise man, who built his house upon the rock. And the rain descended, and the floods came, and the winds blew, and burst against that house; and yet it did not fall, for it had been founded upon the rock. And every one who hears these words of Mine, and does not act upon them, will be like a foolish man, who built his house upon the sand. And the rain descended, and the floods came, and the winds blew, and burst against that house; and it fell, and great was its fall (Matt.7:24–27).

In this brief, picturesque conclusion to what most believe to be the greatest sermon ever preached, Christ sets before His listeners two similar men, two different responses, and two contrasting results. He challenges His listeners with the consequences of their decision in two ways:

- the blessings of obedience
- the blight of the disobedient (passive nonresponder)

Consequences motivate the passive. If a desire to gain the benefits isn't strong enough to motivate to action, Jesus says, then think about your alternative. What's going to happen if you don't? If anything will move the passive nonresponder, avoiding the negative consequences of disobedience will.

We must decide between two possibilities—the price of obedience or the penalty of disobedience. The goal is to move passive listeners to *do* something about the truth; they must not *ignore* it.

You might say, for example, "Husbands, when you love your wife by listening to her concerns, fulfilling her requests, (even if it's washing dishes, doing laundry, or taking out the garbage), blessings abound for everyone—for your wife because she needs to see that she's loved, for your children because of your example, and for you because it's more blessed to give than to receive. Consider the effects when a husband withholds love. Withholding loving deeds to your spouse displeases the Lord. You already know what

Media-Proof Chart #1	
Superior effectiveness	Inferior effectiveness
1. Make points with brevity	1. Drag everything out
2. Keep listeners tracking with you	2. Drop listeners through the cracks
3. Round up strays	3. Let the confused stay so
4. Give spontaneous feedback	4. Hibernate, be oblivious
5. Challenge them with consequences	5. Be academic, no response required

your wife thinks when she perceives a lack of loving concern on your part. Your regrettable example to your children injures their home to be. Men, what you'll gain far surpasses what you'll give."

No wonder Jesus amazed the multitudes and spoke with authority. He challenged people with the positive and negative consequences of obeying the Word of God. Purely academic sermons offering precepts that can be ignored without consequences produce even more passive nonresponders.

Today's preachers can and must penetrate the mind, will, and emotions of this media generation with the message Jesus Christ. At stake are the needs of people and the glory of God.

CHAPTER TEN

Media-Relevant Preaching

W hat's on TV tonight, Dad? may be one of the most often repeated questions in American homes, so let's attempt an answer. But first, in a recent plea for federal legislation the American Academy of Pediatrics cited some illuminating statistics on TV viewers:

Kids aged two to five see about twenty-five hours of TV per week.

Six to eleven-year-olds see about twenty-two hours per week.

Twelve to seventeen-year-olds see about twenty-three hours per week.[1]

What kind of programs are they seeing during this time?

Preschool aged kids have the highest exposure to TV, and the most violent TV is cartoons with 171 incidents of violence per hour.[2]

There are 14,000 sexual references a year on TV.

By age fifteen a teen has seen the violent destruction of 14,000 people.

By age twenty-one a person sees 75,000 incidents of alcohol consumption.
Rape occurs in one out of six films.[3]
A Harvard Study revealed 70 percent of allusions to sexual intercourse were between persons not married to each other.[4]

Most pastors wouldn't hesitate to respond with corrective measures if the Jehovah's Witnesses or Mormons held a Bible study in the living room of a church family. When TV spreads equally poisonous doctrine and openly assaults the purity and the integrity of the body of Christ, faithful pastors *must* reply.

> For the weapons of our warfare are not of the flesh, but divinely powerful for the destruction of fortresses. We are destroying speculations and every lofty thing raised up against the knowledge of God, and we are taking every thought captive to the obedience of Christ (2 Cor. 10:45 NASV).

Admittedly, some TV programming can be good and beneficial. Yet helpful TV is definitely in the minority as compared to harmful TV. The brand of TV that alarms the American Academy of Pediatrics, however, more than qualifies as the "lofty thing raised up against the knowledge of God," which divinely empowered preaching must cast down. But more often than not, preaching falters in this task.

Such distorted perspectives from TV spill over into the thinking and living of the church. The failure of preachers to do preaching that remedies these media-induced ills is inexcusable. The

> "TV creates new and artificial needs in us by altering our attitudes as believers in key areas of Christian concern: the need for moral resolve, the structure of the family, the definition of manhood, the use of possessions and wealth, and even the nature of God Himself."

character and conduct of the church is at stake, and God's side of these issues must be heard. The preacher should proclaim them, but how?

Preachers must adapt their preaching content to expose and replace these media lies and distortions if they hope to meet the needs of the contemporary, media-weary church. Their preaching must become media relevant.

The Real Needs of Our Listeners

As a new pastor just out of seminary, I vividly remember preaching a polished message on biblical prophecy one Sunday and then refereeing a fight between a deacon and his wife during the week. No one in their family could balance the checkbook; their kids were failing in school but they still spent three hours each night in front of the tube. The wife suffered depression from watching the afternoon soaps, while the husband, enamored with sports specials, wondered why Christ made no difference in their home life. My preaching content was hopelessly out of touch with their needs.

Here is the crux of the problem. *TV creates new and artificial needs in us by altering our attitudes as believers in key areas of Christian concern: the need for moral resolve, the structure of the family, the definition of manhood, the use of possessions and wealth, and even the nature of God Himself.*

Scores of homiletics books strangely ignore this major issue. Yet, without question, the most unimpressive message focused on an area of real need will mature believers more effectively than sermons as smooth as silk on secondary topics that make little or no contribution to the Christlikeness of the hearers.

If maturity in Christ is the goal of preaching (Col. 1:27), then content must take priority over form and delivery so that preaching on the right topic is more important than preaching right. Although homileticians like to focus upon the "how tos" of preaching, the priority should be the "what tos."

Of course, a preacher inept in form and delivery is like an incompetent nurse who can't get the proper medication to the right patient in a timely fashion. Yet most patients would rather have the right pill late from an unskilled nurse than swallow the wrong medication from one who is winsome. Preaching with impressive form that lacks the needed content proves at best to be placebo preaching. It's a promise without performance. It may be impressive for a few brief moments in church, yet proves impotent over the long haul during the week when real answers are in demand.

The truth is, TV-saturated people need preaching that is both user-friendly in form and delivery (as explained in chapters 7–10) and relevant to real needs in content (chapter 10). Preaching must retain this needed balance.

Is it possible to biblically diagnose the ills of this media-influenced society? Can pastors find a remedy for TV's mass-media culture? *Yes!* is the answer.

Two Required Steps

Media-relevant preaching requires two steps:

1. Problems must be defined within biblical categories (diagnosis).
2. Solutions offered must be scripturally sound (remedy).

Second Timothy chapter 3 provides the preacher with both a biblical diagnosis and a biblical remedy. Even before the Bible was written, the Holy Spirit obviously knew what conditions would prevail in our day and the challenges we would face. Through the inspiration of the Scriptures, He furnished us with an adequate tool to deal with a world like ours (2 Tim. 3:16). In 2 Timothy 3:1–14 the Spirit describes our society and what's wrong with it. In other words, He gives a biblical diagnosis of our TV-saturated culture. The rest of the chapter, verses 15–17, offers a solution and a hope, that is, a remedy.

The most striking reason to associate media with the prophecy of 2 Timothy 3 is its similarity with the known effects of TV. When comparing God's description of end-of-the-age mass culture with the known effects of TV, the similarities are striking. In fact, the negative consequences of mass media upon society at large follow the expectations of this passage almost as if the prophecy were its blueprint. Secular studies provide such extensive documentation about the unhealthy impact of TV on adults and children that documenting this violent, aggressive, immoral, abusive, end-age behavior may be needless. Yet to prove the point, here's a quote from one of Hollywood's most notable critics, commenting on Michael Jackson's car-smashing video entitled "Black or White."

> [T]he Jackson affair clearly demonstrates that the American people understand that media images influence real-life behavior. The entertainment industry may deny its own impact, but ordinary citizens know better. They know perfectly well that if tens of millions of kids watch repeatedly as Michael Jackson gleefully smashes a car with a crowbar then their own car is that much more likely to get smashed someday—and their own kids are that much more likely to try some smashing. The logic of this assumption is so obvious and inescapable that only the most shameless entertainment executives and their hired academic experts would even attempt to argue against it.[5]

Five Key Media Categories

In each of these following five media categories TV attempts to bring its viewers into conformity with a doctrinal position contrary to the Word of God. When the TV content of these media categories is viewed from a biblical perspective, it reads like a satanic alternative to God's Law for mankind. Media-relevant preaching must overcome these false doctrines by proclaiming the biblical alternatives.

Media-relevant preaching calls for diagnosis and remedy in these five key media categories. Taken as a unit, these "preaching hot spots" possess fascinating characteristics. For example, all five derive from one or more of the Ten Commandments. All have their own identity and a large body of literature in *TV Guide* and other secular writings on TV content. Culturally broad, they cover every society, anywhere, any time. The five key media categories are:

1. God, Christianity, and Spiritual Leaders
2. Man and Masculinity
3. The Family
4. Sex and Violence
5. Possessions and Wealth

The Benefits of Media-Relevant Preaching

Media-relevant preaching will lessen or even reverse the harmful effects of TV. It can rebuild integrity of doctrine and put strength back into the lives of your people in the five key media areas. Such preaching is certain to bring benefits. What are they?

1. God, Christianity, and Spiritual Leaders

The preaching of media-relevant messages on God, Christianity, and spiritual leadership will aid in building attitudes of respect for and lessen criticism of spiritual authority, teach the true worship of our holy God, and encourage more cooperation with the pastor and the church leadership.

2. Man and Masculinity

Real men serve God sacrificially in their churches and families. Media-relevant messages lift up God's ideal man as a servant who sees and meets the needs of others, not as a selfishly-focused consumer. Media-saturated male types who can't seem to fulfill their commitments tend to define masculinity in terms of how many women and how much alcohol they can experience. Preaching that clearly defines biblical masculinity gives men a true standard for manhood and exposes empty media models as worthless and unscriptural rejects.

3. The Family

Preaching on the biblical family and related areas may be the most media-relevant topic possible. God's view of love and commitment protects and produces strong, stable families, gives hope to those who otherwise would divorce, saves many troubled marriages, and enables good marriages to grow stronger. If preachers want to hinder divorce and prevent the next generation of children from tossing marriage out altogether, then they must preach on the family. Marital strife and fractured families destroy individuals, families, churches, and communities.

4. Sex and Violence

Pornography on TV and HBO stirs lust and other illicit desires often resulting in sexual abuse of children, rape, and mistreatment of the elderly. These crimes could be reduced and their harm upon the innocent diminished through media-relevant preaching covering biblical principles appropriate to these issues.

5. Possessions and Wealth

TV commercials are designed to fuel discontent. Preaching that presents God's view of possessions and wealth will help to lighten the debt load upon family finances caused by overspending on a consumptive lifestyle and will instead grow financially free families able to give and to build stable churches. For example, the "gameshow spirit" of our age exemplified on TV can be countered by an exposition of Philippians 4:11–13.

> Not that I speak in respect of want: for I have learned, in whatsoever state I am, therewith to be content. I know both how to be abased, and I know how to abound: every where and in all things I am instructed both to be full and to be hungry, both to abound and to suffer need. I can do all things through Christ which strengtheneth me.

This kind of preaching eases the pressure to spend and promotes contentment with the possessions we have.

Diagnosis: Media's View of God, Christianity, and Spiritual Leaders

Three Greek terms from 2 Timothy 3:3–5 summarize the media's viewpoint: "despisers of the good, lovers of pleasure more than lovers of God," and "having a form of Godliness but denying the power thereof." Together these descriptions portray the antagonism of people of the end times towards God, the church, and all that is good. Nothing defines the true characters of people more than what they love and what they hate. To love pleasure and to hate good speaks volumes.

TV hates Christianity. It scorns religion in any form whether real or perceived. Even a non-Christian like media expert Michael Medved recognizes this antipathy. Here's a quote from his recent best seller *Hollywood vs. America*:

> Universal's woeful experience with the *Last Temptation of Christ* typifies the pervasive and self-destructive hostility

to religion that has taken root in Hollywood. In the ongoing war on traditional values, the assault on organized faith represents the front to which the entertainment industry has most clearly committed itself. On no other issue do the perspectives of the show business elite and those of the public at large differ more dramatically. Time and again, the producers who shape our music, television and popular music have gone out of their way to affront the religious sensibilities of ordinary Americans.[6]

The following remedy charts offer content designed to combat TV's influence in strategic areas. In no sense are they exhaustive, only representative. The goal is to stimulate and motivate the preacher in his own creativity to design preaching series that effectively put off the media models and put on the biblical ones. Every church is a unique composite of individuals and personalities possessing a variety of needs, so that each pastor must decide what to gloss over and what to emphasize. See the five charts which appear on the following 5 pages.

Diagnosis: TV's View of Man and Masculinity

Terms that define end time anthropology found in 2 Timothy 3:2–4 are self lovers, boasters, proud, arrogant, unholy, high minded and conceited. This dismal profile reads like an article from *TV Guide* detailing the lifestyle of many leading stars.

TV glamorizes antiheroes. Psalm 12:8 says, "The wicked walk on every side, when the vilest men are exalted." In other words, if you want to crank out more individuals like Kurt Cobain, then put rock stars on a pedestal. We become like the people we admire. To the degree that we identify with the leading character, we will tend to reflect his attitudes, adopt his values, and imitate his behavior. Thus, pedestalizing negative role models spotlights evil. Whenever this happens, we can expect Psalm 12:8 to be fulfilled.

Preaching must replace these models with the positive and far superior models in the Bible. If our youth are to identify with Abraham, Moses, David, Joseph, Peter, and Paul rather than rock stars, then pastors must preach sermon series that adorn the lives of God's servants. The biblical examples of men and women provide moral patterns for

Remedy: TV's View of God, Christianity, and Spiritual Leaders

Topics and Questions	Outlines	Scripture	Examples
1. The Attributes of God	1. a) God is omniscient—all knowing b) God is omnipresent—everywhere present c) God is omnipotent—all powerful	1. a) Psalm 139 b) Psalm 147:3–4: "He heals the broken hearted and counts the number of the stars." God is both immanent and transcendent.	1. Wisdom, Justice, Greatness, Power, Love, Mercy, Sovereign, Righteous
2. God Is in Your Problem	2. a) God is up to something. b) God is up to something good. c) Find out what it is. d) Get involved in cooperating with God in what He is doing. e) Expect good results.	2. a) Philippians 1:12 b) Genesis 50:20 c) Daniel 6:10–28	2. a) Paul in prison b) Philippians worried c) Joseph in the pit, prison, and coregent of Egypt d) Daniel in the lion's den
3. The First Commandment Is of First Importance	3. Man's First and Greatest Responsibility	3. Matthew 22:34–40—the first and second greatest commandments	3. Christ kept the first commandment (John 10:17–18)
4. The Church, the Body of Christ	4. Eternal Foundation in Christ: Universal scope, Loftey goal, Glorious renewal, Effective armour—EULOGE[7]	4. a) Revelation 2 and 3 b) Matthew 16:18—"I will build My church." c) Ephesians—Study the glory of the church	4. Seven churches of Asia
5. Persecution for the Sake of the Message in the Last Days	5. Right perspective Toward Pastors and Christian Leaders	5. a) 1 Timothy—Study of church order and function b) 1 Peter—Book study on responding to hostility by culture c) 1 Corinthians 4:1–6 d) Hebrews 13:17	5. Paul stoned at Lystra—Acts 14:19; Peter imprisoned at Jerusalem—Acts 12:3–5; 2 Corinthians 6:1–10—Pastors everywhere should expect difficulty

Chart #1

Remedy: TV's View of Man and Masculinity

Topics and Questions	Outlines	Scripture	Examples
1. What makes a man a man?	1. Marks of manhood: The false and the true—Mr. Macho, Superjock, Soldier without a soul, Gender Blenders	1. 1 Corinthians 13:11—become a man, be mature Ephesians 4:14—Be no more children: be consistent	1. False models—Eastwood, Schwartznegger, Stallone, M. Jackson
2. Feminized males in America.	2. The curse of the passive male—"Mother runs the family, Daddy is a wimp." "How to grow a homosexual son."	2. Judges 4:7—"If you go I will go, but if you will not go then I will not go." Barak, the Ninny Philippians 2:1–7	2. Moses, Abraham, David, Job, Daniel, Paul, Timothy
3. Models of masculinity from the Bible.	3. Traits of biblical masculinity—servanthood, humility, responsibility, self-control, love example	3. Mark 10:32–45—Christ's model of leadership	3. Christ: The measure of men
4. Real men don't.	4. Alcohol, sex, fighting, money	4. Ephesians 5:25ff 1 Thessalonians 4:1–8 Genesis 13:5–9 Acts 4:36–37	4. Self-control: Joshua, unselfish love: Abraham, true meekness: Barnabas

Chart #2

Remedy: TV's View of the Family

Topics and Questions	Outlines	Scripture	Examples
1. God's blueprint for marriage	1. One man, one woman, one lifetime	1. Genesis 2:24—"They two shall be one flesh."	1. Christ and the church
2 The role of the husband	2. Lover, learner, leader	2. Ephesians 5:25—"Husbands love your wives." 1 Peter 3:7a—"Husbands, live with your wife in an understanding way."	2. Joseph—Mary's husband (Matt. 1:11–25)
3. The role of the wife	3. Creative counterpart and submissive helper. What do you do when you think your husband is wrong.	3. Genesis 2:18—". . . a helper suitable." 1 Peter 3:1–6	3. Ruth—loyalty, Ruth 1:16–18 Abigail—1 Samuel 25:3
4. The parent-child relationship	4. Your goal as a parent: "Bring them up in the discipline and instruction of the Lord."	4. Ephesians 6:4 Proverbs 6:20–23	4. 2 Timothy 1:5—Timothy and Eunice, Lois: Successful single parents
5. The four rules of communication	5. Be Honest; Keep Current; Attack the Problem, Not the Person; Act, Don't React	5. Ephesians 4:25–32	5. Galatians 2:11ff—Paul confronts Peter
6. Discipline with dignity	6. Raising children who are a match for their time.	6. Proverbs 13:1 Proverbs 29:17 Proverbs 23:13–14	6. 1 Timothy 4:12–15—Paul and Timothy

Chart #3

Remedy: TV's View of Sex and Violence

Topics and Questions	Outlines	Scripture	Examples
1. The biblical view of the sexual relationship within marriage	1. a) Sex within marriage is holy and good b) Sexual relations are to be regular and continuous c) Sexual relations are to be equal and reciprocal	1. 1 Corinthians 7:1–7; Hebrews 13:4; Proverbs 5:18–19	1. Song of Solomon
2. God's view of sex outside of marriage (fornication and adultery) 3. Biblical love	2. How to distinguish between love and lust 3. a) Love is not feeling first b) Love is giving, not getting c) Love is action d) Christ, our mode.	2. 1 Thessalonians 4:1–8; 1 Corinthians 6:15–20; Matthew 19:1–12; 2 Samuel 13:1–18. 3. 1 Corinthians 13:1–8; 1 John 4:7–21	2. Samson and Delilah Amnon rapes Tamar 3. Jesus Christ
4. What the Bible says about dating relationships and standards 5. What to do when you're angry	4. How to draw up biblical dating standards 5. a) All anger isn't sinful b) Four times when anger becomes sinful c) Handling anger biblically. Genesis 1:27–28; 1 Corinthians 7:1–7	4. 1 Corinthians 10:31—" … do all for the glory of God"—this includes dating relationships 5. Genesis 24:1–67; Ephesians 4:26; Proverbs 14:17, 29; Proverbs 15:1, 18; Proverbs 16:32; Proverbs 19:19; Romans 12:17–22; 1 Peter 2:17–22	4. Abraham gets a wife for Isaac (Rebecca) 5. Galatians 2:11–16—Paul and Peter
6. Returning good for evil	6. How to really turn the other cheek	6. Genesis 50:20	6. Joseph and his brothers

Chart #4

Remedy: TV's View of Possessions and Wealth

Topics and Questions	Outlines	Scripture	Examples
1. Rethinking biblical stewardship	1. Wealth, possessions, and eternity	1. Exodus 20:17; Matthew 6:24; 1 Timothy 5:5–12; James 5:1–6	1. Rich young ruler—Luke 18:18–30; Abraham, Genesis 14:20, gave tithes of all
2. Stewardship not ownership view of life	2. a) God owns it all b) He entrusts to us all we have c) We are responsible to increase not diminish d) God, the owner, may call us into account at anytime	2. Matthew 25:14–30—The parable of the talents 1 Peter 4:10—All believers are stewards 2 Corinthians 5:10—All believers must appear before the Judgment Seat of Christ	2. Woman with the alabaster box of ointment, Matthew 26:6–13; David's sacrificial example of giving in 2 Samuel 24:18–25
3. How much is enough?	3. Contentment vs. covetousness Greed	3. 1 Timothy 6:6–10; Hebrews 13:5; Psalm 84:11	3. Paul—lost all things (Phil. 3:8), abounded and suffered in all things (Phil. 4:12–13), possesses all things (Phil. 4:18–19)
4. Wrong way to riches	4. Debt, the emptiness of materialism	4. Proverbs 15:27; Romans 13:8; Proverbs 22:7; Proverbs 10:2	4. Gehazi—2 Kings 5:26–27; Achan—Joshua 7:19–26; Ananias and Sapphira—Acts 5:1–11; Judas—Matthew 27:3–9
5. Discovering the grace of giving	5. a) Grace giving is sacrificial b) Grace giving is spontaneous c) Grace giving is selfless d) Grace giving is systematic e) Grace giving is sincere	5. 2 Corinthians 8 and 9; 1 Corinthians 16:1–3	5. Widow's mite—Mark 12:41–44; Early church in Acts 4:33–35; Cornelius in Acts 10

Chart #5

character and conduct and place a measuring stick in our hands for personal growth. We become like the people we look up to.

Diagnosis: TV's View of the Family

Six Greek words from 2 Timothy 3 accurately describe the media view of the family—disobedient to parents (verse 2), trucebreakers, irreconcilable, unforgiving (verse 4), brutal (verse 3), and incontinent, without self-control (verse 3).

Disobedient to parents relates to the parent-child relationship. TV's children aren't noted for obedience to parents. "Father Knows Best" from the 1950s could be characterized in the 90s as "Father Knows Nothing." What motive have children to obey the masculine leader in the family when usually he can't seem to keep his act together? The second category, irreconcilable, etc., describes someone with whom it is impossible to get along, for whom divisions are the norm, who refuses to be brought together. Divorce, domestic violence, and conflict between husbands and wives fit here. The next term, brutal, characterizes the physically violent and abusive. Finally, without self-control identifies the sexually immoral for whom illicit sex is more appealing than sex within marriage.

The media definition of a family seldom reflects God's divine standard, one man and one woman for one lifetime. Even making allowances for legitimate and unavoidable single-parent family situations, God's definition will be seen less than one time in twenty on the so-called family programs.

"What is a father?" was once questioned by the media. It has now been superceded by a more alarming question, "Is a father even necessary?" In the wake of the now famous Murphy Brown-Vice President Quayle debacle this burning issue must not be lost. *Yes!* is God's emphatic answer to this new question. His plan for the family always includes a father and a husband; yet one could die of old age waiting to hear this truth on TV. Does TV really present this 2 Timothy 3 view of the family or are we overstating the case? Once again, an expert from the world of TV speaks to the issue with authority about the media view of the family. From *Hollywood vs. America*, Part III, entitled "The Assault on the Family":

Before 1970, 38 percent of all shows that depicted nonmarital sexuality clearly condemned it as morally unacceptable. More recently, only 7 percent of the shows that portray such affairs present them in a disapproving light, while 41 percent endorse them without qualification.

This peculiar notion that marriage and fun cannot comfortably coexist is by now deeply embedded in the television culture: the only sort of steamy sex that seems to be forbidden on the small screen is the kind that might connect two married people to each other. Al and Peg Bundy of the Fox Network's *Married . . . with Children* sitcom represent Hollywood's image of the typical husband and wife, as she complains endlessly—and graphically—about her nonexistent sex life.

In the "Spring Sweeps" period of 1991 (April 28–May 25), researchers for the American Family Association logged a total of 615 instances of sexual activity depicted or discussed on prime-time shows. By a margin of thirteen to one (571 to 44) these references favored sex outside of marriage over intimate relations between life partners.[8]

What effect do all these scenes have on children? TV banishes childhood. 1 Corinthians 13:11, 14:20, and Ephesians 4:14 tell us some of the differences between adults and children. Principally, the differences involve knowledge and experience. God's desire is that these two components of maturity grow together, as in the life of Christ described in Luke 2:52. But TV is an open-admission medium. It does not discriminate whether or not its viewers are six or sixty. Through TV children can be exposed to more violence and evil in one week than they would normally experience in a lifetime. This exposure prematurely accelerates the growth and maturation process, throwing the child into an "experience gap," where his or her TV knowledge races far ahead of personal experience. The result is a child of twelve who is going on twenty-five, a child left struggling with a puzzling loss of innocence and a handful of half-truths and unanswered questions.

Diagnosis: Media's View of Sex and Violence

Six terms from the list of nineteen in 2 Timothy 3 describe either sex, violence, or both: brutal, reckless, revilers, abusive, lovers of self, and without self-control.

Mass media's glorification of sex and violence is widely acknowledged. Newspapers carry feature stories about the harm being done to children; radio talk show hosts interview call-ins who complain about violence. Psychologists publish prodigious studies citing the evidence that TV violence is harmful to children, but nobody does anything about it. This is largely true because only the U.S. Congress through the Federal Communications Commission has the power to legislate changes in the laws governing TV programming.

> "Since much of TV's content presents unbiblical responses to life, TV amounts to a resource center for wrong responses."

Medved supports the extent to which violence infests TV. Violent messages are no longer limited to a few feature films per year; they assault average American teenagers in the course of the twenty-six hours of TV and the ten hours of music they consume each week. Can anyone doubt that this sort of steady exposure exerts more influence on the mass audience than those isolated instances of brutal and controversial films that have turned up from time to time in Hollywood's past?[9]

Exposure to TV does indeed desensitize us to violence. Exposure to violent scenes on TV and in movies is a key factor in stimulating youth violence. Many prime-time network dramas contain some act of physical, mental, or verbal violence, and the incidents increase in late evening programming. The effects of this programming upon society at large are inescapable.

There is now a wave of crime that police experts call "copy-cat crimes." Such crime happens all across America. In Hartford City, Indiana, four men chose a home at random and blasted four brothers to death with shotguns. They later testified that viewing the TV version of the Charles Manson murders, "Helter Skelter," had influenced them in committing the crime.[10] TV supplies persons having criminal desires with ideas and strategies that further enable them to carry out their evil plans. Romans 13:14 warns not to give wrong desires a strategy for fulfillment.

Since much of TV's content presents unbiblical responses to life, TV amounts to a resource center for wrong responses. Why should believers spend hours viewing examples of how to respond unbiblically?

Diagnosis: TV's View of Possessions and Wealth

Included in the list of the endtime's view of money and belongings are the sins of covetousness, verse 2, (which is literally "the love of silver") and unthankfulness and ingratitude, verse 2, which seem to exist in inverse proportion to one's possessions. As Shakespeare so aptly observes in *King Lear*,

> O ingratitude thou marble-hearted fiend. How sharper than a serpent's tooth it is to have a thankless child.

Can anyone doubt that media is responsible for propagating this mentality? TV preaches that materialism means happiness. Being content with "such things as you have" takes considerable effort. But Hebrews 13:5 reminds us that this is the command of God to all believers. Paul had to learn to be content in any state according to Philippians 4:11. Does TV help us to learn contentment? Where does the pressure to get more and more come from? Primarily from the constant hammering of commercials and their relentless goal to make us discontent with our standard of living, whatever it may be. TV constitutes a competing influence against contentment.

To overcome the tidalwave of greed and selfishness that TV fosters, God's people must be convinced that biblical stewardship is required. If pastors want stability in their churches, preaching must counter the awesome forces of dissatisfaction and the continual desire for more. Remedies for media materialism will encourage believers to avoid a consumptive lifestyle and instead to adopt a *stewardship* rather than an *ownership* view of life.

Don't roll over and play dead, instead counterstrike. Roll up your sleeves and be God's mouthpiece to a needy church and community. In all likelihood they'll never hear these divine standards from TV. Preachers must proclaim it.

CHAPTER ELEVEN

Media-Proof Your Messages

The goal of this book is effective preaching to programmed people. To achieve effective preaching, two questions were raised and answered, "What has TV done to preaching?" and "What should preaching do about TV?" The answers, principles, and procedures offered, however, will provide little help apart from implementation by the preacher himself. Becoming an effective preacher to programmed people, therefore, requires a process of evaluation and change over a period of time. In order to achieve this goal, preachers need a concrete way to objectively examine their performance against a predetermined standard. This is where the **P.I.P.P.** comes in, the **P**ersonalized **I**mprovement **P**rogram for **P**reachers.

The P.I.P.P.

The **P.I.P.P.** program allows the busy pastor to develop a preaching format for change at his own pace. It involves three easy steps. One is to have his Sunday morning sermons taped by a VCR recorder. Next, the preacher must watch his message on TV while filling out the following evaluation guide. Finally, he decides which changes are to take place first, second, and so on, and then draws up a plan for change.

This sermon evaluation form cannot take the place of other regular homiletical evaluations, but it can increase the effectiveness of the preacher upon his media- saturated listeners.

Most churches have someone in the congregation with a video recorder, i.e. a camcorder. Have your message taped, then at your leisure view the VCR tape of your sermon with the evaluation form in hand and check off the appropriate areas. It is best to familiarize yourself with the twenty categories ahead of time by referring back to the explanation given in the appropriate chapter. As you watch yourself on the tape, be honest; tapes don't lie. Imagine yourself as a member of the congregation, and realize that this is what they see and hear every Sunday. If no camcorder is available, then give the following form to your wife or to a friend to fill in during your message, then follow the same procedure as you would with the tape.

After filling in the evaluation guide, review the information and prioritize the areas you checked under "needs improvement," then choose one area and plan steps for change. You decide the level of priority to be assigned to each area. Work on the areas where you are most highly motivated or that would bring the biggest improvement. Be prayerful and make it personal. For example, if your form shows twelve areas where your preaching is O.K., set these aside and work instead on the areas you checked under "needs improvement." Perhaps you had seven areas needing improvement, prioritize them from one to seven. Then work on the top one or two. It's usually best to work on changes within one category (structure-form, content, delivery) at a time rather than all three categories; that is, work on delivery in one sermon, form the next, and content in the following message. Attempting to make too many changes all at once can be a recipe for discouragement.

Evaluation Categories

For ease of evaluation the twenty media areas have been summarized into the three standard homiletical categories.

1. *Form* is anything that involves the way the content of the sermon is structured, such as the size and shape of

Preaching to Programmed People
P.I.P.P. Evaluation Guide

	O.K.	Needs Improvement
I. Form (Sermon Structure)		
Chapter 7: TV's Achilles' Heel/Preaching's Power		
1. Be Spontaneous	☐	☐
Chapter 8: The Distinctive Power of Preaching		
2. Personalized applications— targeting and shaping	☐	☐
3. Use listener profile information	☐	☐
Chapter 9: Purge Boredom Factors		
4. Paint images using words	☐	☐
Chapter 10: Preaching to Programmed People		
5. Brevity	☐	☐
6. Keep listeners tracking with you	☐	☐
7. Round up strays	☐	☐
8. Give audience feedback	☐	☐
9. Consequences explained	☐	☐
II. Content		
Chapter 6: Capitalize on TV		
10. Commercials	☐	☐
11. Movies and Films	☐	☐
12. Sports	☐	☐
13. News Headlines	☐	☐
Chapter 9: Purge Boredom Factors		
14. Be Real—The A-B-C Method	☐	☐
Chapter 11 Media-Relevant Preaching		
15. God, Christianity, and Spiritual Leaders	☐	☐
16. Man and Masculinity	☐	☐
17. The Family	☐	☐
18. Sex and Violence	☐	☐
19. Possessions and Wealth	☐	☐
III. Delivery		
Chapter 7: TV's Achilles' Heel/Preaching's Power		
20. Be spontaneous	☐	☐
Chapter 9: Purge Boredom Factors		
21. Be mobile in delivery	☐	☐
Chapter 10 Preaching to Programmed People		
22. Use sounds	☐	☐

the introduction and conclusion, the number of points in the body of the sermon, or the relationship of the major points to each other. There are eight areas of evaluation on how to structure the sermon for maximum impact including applications, painting word pictures, or shaping the conclusion.

2. *Content* is the information comprising the subject material of the sermon itself. There are ten areas of evaluation in this category. The first five are nonspecific, that is, they can be used on any topic or subject the preacher may choose. The second five target specific content relative to media.

3. *Delivery* includes the style in which the preacher presents his sermon to his audience. The elements of style involve voice inflection, word choice, gestures, mood, and in general those distinctive features of the preacher that define his personality and identity him as a communicator. Movement and sound in preaching, as with TV, are the raw materials of delivery.

How to Use the P.I.P.P.

Let's say, for example, the top three areas from your needs improvement list were:

1. Be mobile in delivery—use meaningful movement
2. Paint word pictures
3. Personalize applications by targeting and shaping

On the first Sunday instead of remaining at the pulpit for the entire sermon, move from one side to the other at strategically preplanned points. During the message, back up and give the pulpit some room, use voice inflection, loosen up those broom handle arms with content-appropriate motions. Wake up your church! Preachers must work to avoid the sleepy church syndrome.

On the second Sunday work on painting word pictures by following the steps on page 94 and get ideas from the chart on page 95. The following Sunday prevent channel surfing by personalized applications through targeting and shaping instead of talking to generic persons who don't really exist. Begin to talk to real people where they live. Remember to target people groups in the audience. Use descriptive phrases such as "discouraged homemaker, if you're tired of staying at home with your children and you think life is passing you by, remember what Paul said . . .." See media charts 1 and 2 on pages 140–141 for ideas.

P.I.P.P. for media-proofing messages

1. Tape your preaching.
2. View the tape and fill in the evaluation guide.
3. Prioritize the "needs improvement" list.
4. Choose one area to improve.
5. Plan the changes.
6. Preach!

Work on the current area until the changes are satisfactory, then go on to next item on the list. Each week you can decide to stay with an area or move on, always at your own speed.

I've followed this procedure for years and I promise you, if no one else sees a difference in your preaching, *you will,* and that's reason enough to continue. But *others will see and hear the difference.* Any area—form, content, or delivery—can be improved by this method. It gives the preacher a personalized plan for change at his own pace. The benefits far outweight the costs. Whatever your individual need or congregational setting may be, practice and hard work make a difference. As Paul told Timothy in 1 Timothy 4:15, "Meditate upon these things; give thyself wholly to them; that thy profiting may appear to all."

By following these steps you will become an effective preacher to programmed people.

CHAPTER TWELVE

Media-Proof Your Church

After the preacher has done the hard work of self evaluation, he should move on to the next step—congregational evaluation. Using the **P.I.P.P.** will aid in the development of the kind of preaching skills necessary to media-proof your message. Those skills, however, must be applied to your particular congregation in order to media-proof your church.

Measure "TV-Conditioning" in Your Church

The people in the pews are the other half of the equation. Therefore, we must have an accurate measurement of TV's effects on them, and the following quiz supplies that information. In or before Sunday school or during or after Sunday morning church, hand out the following "Seven Question Quiz." (It only takes five minutes to complete.) Evaluating the quiz results will tell you a lot (maybe more than you want to know) about how people perceive your preaching and the extent of TV-conditioning in your church. This information will guide your choice of message topics for effective preaching to programmed people.

SEVEN QUESTION QUIZ

1. How many hours of TV do you watch a day ?_____ a week_____?

2. Rank your favorite shows.
   (Most favorite = 1, Neutral = 2, Dislike = 3)
   ___Feature Films
   ___Dramatic Series
   ___Situation Comedies (Sitcoms)
   ___Public Television
   ___Soaps
   ___Arts and Nature
   ___Sports
   ___News

Circle the appropriate response to the following questions:

3. Is preaching more or less relevant to real life than your favorite show from question 2?   more \ less

4. Is preaching more or less exciting than TV?   more \ less

5. Is preaching easier or harder to follow than TV?   easier \ harder

6. Does TV strengthen or weaken your convictions as a Christian?   strengthen \ weaken

   In what areas is TV weakening your convictions as a Christian?

   _____
   _____
   _____
   _____

7. Overall, does TV help or hurt your understanding of preaching?   help \ hurt

---

Evaluation

Now tally the results and choose an area to work on. The results of this quiz will enable you to determine the extent of TV-conditioning within the members of your congregation and how it affects their responses to preaching. For example, if a majority of persons said, "TV is more relevant to life than preaching," you need to use one of those five key media topics in chapter 10 and do more *media-relevant preaching.* Or perhaps they said, "TV is weakening my convictions as a Christian." Their answers to question 6, "In what areas is TV weakening my convictions as a Christian," will allow you to target your preaching content to prop up their sagging beliefs. Perhaps, according to many, "Preaching is harder to follow than TV." This indicates a need for the principles in chapter 9 on how to keep your listeners with you and get them back when they're lost.

If using the survey is not expedient in church, try a leadership meeting or with Sunday school teachers or with some other small group. This survey enables the preacher to grow in the most needed areas rather than guessing or choosing at random.

Prioritize Congregational Needs

Prioritizing congregational needs enables the preacher to plan the kind of preaching that will media-proof his church. For example, question 6 of the survey indicates that an area of great need is preaching on the biblical family. Thus, preaching on the biblical family becomes a first-level "Prioritized Congregational Need."

First see the remedy chart on page 123 for ideas and then plan a four week series on the family. For example, the first Sunday's sermon could be on God's blueprint for marriage; second Sunday, the role of the husband; third, the role of the wife; fourth, how to communicate, and so on. Targeting your preaching toward specific needs that have been previously identified will assist the nurturing of media-proof churches.

Prioritized Congregational Need: Level Two—If the survey indicates a significant percentage of the congregation (15 to 20 percent) said preaching is both harder to follow and less exciting than TV, the possibility is strong that the preacher should work hard on purging those boredom factors. See media charts 1 and 2 on pages 140–141 for ideas.

Prioritized Congregational Need: Level Three—The quiz results from question 3 indicate many believers don't consider preaching as relevant as TV. These hearers are classic nonresponders. Only when they're challenged with the consequences of their passivity will they see the relevance of the Scriptures to their lives. See media-proof charts 1 and 2 for ideas. An example of the first two of a four-week series of sermons designed to media-proof these nonresponders might look like this:

The first Sunday: What happens when believers don't share their faith? Show the consequences of weak evangelism. What happens when they do? Show the blessings of leading the nonchurched to Christ.

The second Sunday: The consequences of prayerlessness verses the blessings of answered prayer—motivation for the passive to put off prayerlessness and put on prayerfulness.

After planning these steps for change in the prioritized area, all that is left is to preach!

Media-Proof Chart #1	
Superior Effectiveness	**Inferior Effectiveness**
1. Make points with brevity	1. Ramble, drag everything out
2. Keep listeners tracking with you	2. Drop listeners through the cracks
3. Round up strays	3. Let the confused stay so
4. Give spontaneous feedback	4. Hibernate, be oblivious
5. Challenge them with the consequences	5. Be academic, no response required

Media-Proof Chart #2	
Superior Effectiveness	**Inferior Effectiveness**
1. Personalize applications through targeting and shaping	1. Impersonal applications
2. Be mobile; use meaningful movement	2. Immobile, frozen
3. Paint images: use concrete, detailed word pictures	3. No images, picture poor
4. Employ legitimate TV content	4. Shared knowledge unused
5. Media-relevant preaching	5. Out of touch preaching

Steps for Media-Proofing Your Church

1. Measure congregational needs by the Seven Question Quiz
2. Prioritize the needs list
3. Decide on a preaching plan for change
4. Preach
5. Evaluate changes. If satisfactory, go on to next item on list; if not, continue to work on the current area.

Conclusion

Place yourself in this scene. It's Sunday morning and the services have just ended. As you stand in the foyer of your church, shaking hands and thanking your people as they leave, your eye picks up a group of teenagers coming toward you. It's those youth who sit in the front of the church taking notes while you preach. They ask you for your sermon outline.

At home they tell their parents, "Our pastor is terrific! His sermons are exciting and easy to understand! We look forward to hearing him!"

Then you hear a soft and gentle voice. This sweet elderly lady encourages you almost every Sunday when she says, "Thank you, Pastor, for that fine sermon. Listening to you preach is about the only time I can stay awake for more than twenty minutes after I sit down."

Abruptly you feel something squeezing your hand and

see your arm acting like a pump handle as Bob and Claudia, a committed Christian couple, shake your hand and introduce you to a nonchurched friend they have finally succeeded in bringing to church. Their guest responds enthusiasitically and gives you the impression that he will definitely be back next Sunday.

In a silent foyer you prepare to go home when a godly church leader approaches and rejoices with you about this year's increase in church attendance. "People just can't stay away from sound teaching when their needs are being met, Pastor. These are the Last Days you know."

Everyone lingers in the foyer to encourage one another and fellowship together. The same scenes are played out after the PM service, except several small groups go over to a friend's house to discuss the application of the evening message and how they can change as a result of what they've learned.

Addendum

Chapter Discussion Questions

Chapter One
1. What three categories of persons in your church watch the most TV? List them in order.
2. List four reasons pastors should be concerned about TV's impact on preaching.

Chapter Two
1. How does TV change the way people hear your preaching?
2. Name five major differences between TV and preaching.

Chapter Three
1. TV's form of communication dictates the role of its viewers—true or false?
2. List three ways TV moves people away from the preaching model.
3. Why are these TV-induced changes harmful to preaching?
4. Define "The Sunday Morning Hurdle."

Chapter Four
1. What does TV Tom's sermon evaluation form look like?
2. List the "Big Seven" in order.
3. Define these terms: grazing/channel surfing, decontextualization, the jarring effect.

Chapter Five
1. Give seven reasons why TV cannot disciple its viewers.
2. What two requirements for worship does TV fail to meet?
3. What contrasts and comparisons can be drawn between real and televised preaching?

Chapter Six
1. What makes TV an effective source for quotes and illustrations?
2. Name four TV categories that capitalize on the principle of shared knowledge.

Chapter Seven
1. List four ways preaching is superior to TV.
2. Explain targeting and shaping.
3. What two questions must be answered in order first to target and shape and then to make application?
4. Why is this method of applying truth effective for TV-conditioned mentalities?

Chapter Eight
1. Name the three boredom factors and their solutions.
2. Give three reasons why moving images capture the attention of viewers.
3. List two examples of meaningful movements.
4. What is a "word picture"?
5. Why should preaching begin with real-life experience?
6. How can the A-B-C method help preachers choose relevant sermon content?

Chapter Nine
1. Why is media-relevant preaching just as important as correcting the false doctrines of the cults?
2. Is it possible to address media issues from a biblical point of view?
3. List five benefits of media-relevant preaching.
4. What are the five key media categories?
5. Identify the scriptural remedies for each of these media categories.

Chapter Ten
1. Rambling, redundant, and wordy sermons are guaranteed to bore the TV generation. Why?
2. Name four ways to round up strays.
3. Cite two ways to motivate the passive nonresponder to action.

Chapter Eleven
1. Explain the **P.I.P.P.**
2. How can it help media-proof your messages?
3. What steps can be taken to media-proof your church?

Endnotes

Chapter 1
1. *Information Please Almanac* (U.S. Department of Education; Neilsen Media Research, 1994).
2. Malcom Muggeridge. *Christ and the Media* (Grand Rapids: William B. Eerdmans Publishing Co., 1977), 23.
3. Mark Selepica. "Preaching and Evangelism." Doctoral diss., The Master's Seminary, Escondido, Calif., August, 1992.
4. V. Doner Colonel. *The Responsible Parents Guide to TV* (Lafayette, La.: Huntington House, Inc., 1988), 19.

Chapter 2
1. Neil Postman. *Amusing Ourselves to Death: Public Discourse in the Age of Show Business* (New York: Viking Penquin Inc., 1985), 87.
2. Edward Jay Whetmore. *Mediamerica: Form, Content, and Consequences of Mass Communication* (Belmont, Calif.: Wadsworth Inc., 1985), 10.
3. Jerry Mander. *Four Arguments for the Elimination of Television* (New York: William Morrow and Company, Inc., 1978), 208–209.
4. Marshal McLuhan. *The Medium Is the Message: An Inventory of Effects* (New York: Random House, 1967), 8.

5. Quentin J. Schultze. *Redeeming Television: How TV Changes Christians—How Christians Can Change TV* (Downers Grove, Ill.: InterVarsity Press, 1992), 94–95.

Chapter 3
1. Postman. *Amusing Ourselves to Death*, 152.

Chapter 4
1. Muggeridge. *Christ and the Media*, 23.
2. Postman. *Amusing Ourselves to Death*, 87.
3. *American Behavioral Scientist* 31, no. 3 (January–February 1988): 327–40.
4. Dr. Joyce Brothers. "The Shows That Will Make You Feel Better," *TV Guide* (12 March 1989): 35–39.
5. "A Comic's Comic," *TV Guide* (February 1993): 43–47.
6. "Laughter: An empirical test of some reversal theory hypotheses," *Scandinavian Journal of Psychology* 28, no. 3 (1987): 189–98.
7. Morris B. Holbrook and Rajeev Batra. "Assessing the Role of Emotions as Mediators of Consumer Responses to Advertising," *Journal of Consumer Research* 1, no. 3 (December 1987): 404–20.
8. Bill Hybels. *Mastering Contemporary Preaching* (Portland, Ore.: Multnomah Press, 1989), 31.
9. *Empirical Studies of the Arts* 5, no. 1 (1987): 31–46.
10. *USA Today* (23 June 1992): 8.
11. John R. Schallow and Robert D., McIlinraith. "Is Viewing TV Really Bad for Your Imagination?" *Imagination, Cognition and Personality* 6, no. 1 (1986–1987): 25–42.
12. Warren Wiersbe. *The Integrity Crisis* (Nashville: Nelson, 1988), 97.
13. "Television and Passivity," *Rutgers University Research Society* 28, no. 1 (November–December 1990): 3.
14. David L. Groves. "Sport and Leisure and Its Use in Television Programs and Commercials: A Model," *Psychology: A Quarterly Journal of Human Behavior* 24, no. 1–2 (1987): 13–21.
15. Os Guiness. *No God But God* (Chicago: Moody, 1992), 172.

16. Postman. *Amusing Ourselves to Death,* 87.
17. Mander. *Four Arguments,* 166.

Chapter 5

1. Guiness. *No God But God,* 162.
2. Ibid.
3. Wiersbe. *Integrity Crisis,* 99.
4. Tony Sargent. *The Sacred Anointing* (Hodder & Stoughton: London, 1994), 56.
5. Jay Adams. *Preaching with Purpose* (Phillipsburg, NJ.: Presbyterian and Reformed Publishing Co., 1982), 13.
6. Wiersbe. *Integrity Crisis,* 102.
7. Leith Anderson. *A Church for the 21st Century* (Minneapolis: Bethany House Publishers, 1992), 57.
8. Quentin Schultze. *The Agony of Deceit: TV and Evangelism: Unequally Yoked?* (Chicago: Moody Press, 1990), 192.

Part II

1. John MacArthur. "Now a word from our sponsor," *Masterpiece Magazine* (Spring 1989).

Chapter 6

1. Neilsen Media Research. *The Information Please Almanac.* (Houghton and Mifflin Co., 1992), 736-37.

Chapter 7

1. Lewis Sperry Chafer. *Chafer's Systematic Theology,* vol. 1 (Grand Rapids: Kregel, 1993), 58.
2. *Broadcasting in America* (Boston: Houghton Mifflin Company, 1990), 276.
3. Adams. *Preaching with Purpose,* 34–41.
4. Haddon Robinson. *Mastering Contemporary Preaching* (Portland, Ore.: Multinomah, 1989), 20–21.
5. Timothy Keller. "A Model for Preaching," *The Journal of Biblical Counseling* (Glenside, Penn.), 39.

Chapter 8

1. Michael Shaara. *The Killer Angels* (New York: Ballantine Books, 1974), xvi–xxi.
2. Quentin Schultze. "TV and Evangelism: Unequally

Yoked?" in *The Agony of Deceit: What Some TV Preachers Are Really Teaching* ed. Michael Horton (Chicago: Moody Press, 1990), 193.

Chapter 9
1. Max Lucado. *When God Whispers Your Name* (Irving, Tx.: Word, 1994).
2. Adams. *Preaching with Purpose*, 95.

Chapter 10
1. Neilson Media Research. *Information Please Almanac* (1991), 737.
2. Peterson and Hellmich. "Kids Need Help Watching TV," *Chronicle–Tribune* (March 29, 1992): 15.
3. Phil Phillips and Joan Hake Robie. *Horror and Violence: The Deadly Duo in the Media* (Lancaster, Penn.: Starburst Publishers, 1988), 13.
4. Donald E. Wildmon. *The Home Invaders* (Wheaton, Ill.: Victor Books, 1985), 35.
5. Michael Medved. *Hollywood vs. America* (New York: HarperCollins/Zondervan, 1992), 14.
6. Medved. *Hollywood vs. America*, 50.
7. William Hendrikssen. *New Testament Commentary* (Grand Rapids: Baker, 1967), 63–64.
8. Medved. *Hollywood vs. America*, 95.
9. Medved. *Hollywood vs. America*, 183.
10. Phil Phillips and Joan Hake Robie. *Horror and Violence* (Lancaster, Penn.: Starburst Publishers, 1988), 176.